ACTOR'S SCRIPT
Table of Contents

Welcome to the Theater

Congratulations! You'll be working with your **creative team** and fellow **cast** members to put on a **musical**. Before you begin **rehearsals**, there are some important things you should know. This book is your **script**. Whether putting on a school production or rehearsing a professional show, every **actor**, **director**, and **stage manager** works from a script. Your Actor's Script contains additional information for this musical, like this introduction and two glossaries. You can look up any bold words in the Actor's Glossary at the back of this book. Be sure to take good care of your script and take notes wit a pencil since what you'll be doing onstage can change during rehearsals.

One of the first things you'll need to learn is what to call the various areas of the stage. Since most stages used to be **raked**, or tilted down toward the **house** where the audience sits, the term **downstage** is still used to refer to the area closest to the audience, and **upstage** is used to refer to the area farthest from the audience. **Stage left** and **stage right** are from the actor's perspective when facing the audience. This diagram shows how to use these terms to label nine different parts of the stage.

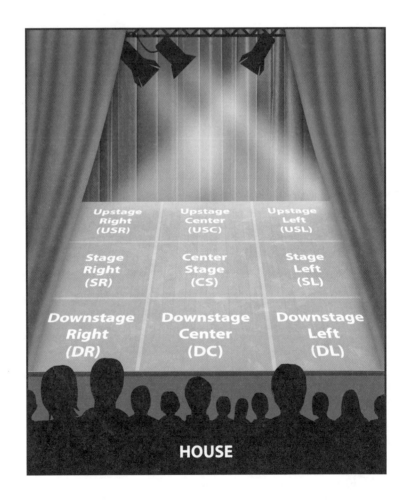

Upstage Right (USR)	Upstage Center (USC)	Upstage Left (USL)
Stage Right (SR)	Center Stage (CS)	Stage Left (SL)
Downstage Right (DR)	Downstage Center (DC)	Downstage Left (DL)

HOUSE

What to Expect During Rehearsals

You will be performing a musical, a type of **play** that tells a story through music, **choreography**, and **dialogue**. Because there are so many parts of a musical, most shows have more than one **author**. The **composer** writes the music and usually works with a **lyricist**, who writes the **lyrics**, or words, for the songs. The **book writer** writes the dialogue (spoken words, or **lines**) and the **stage directions**, which tell the actors what to do onstage and which music cues to listen for. If the book writer and lyricist are the same person, she is often referred to as the **librettist**, since the book and lyrics together are referred to as the **libretto**.

Your director will plan rehearsals so that the cast is ready to give its best performance on **opening night**! Remember to warm up before each rehearsal so that your mind, body, and voice are ready to go. Every rehearsal process is a little bit different, but here is an idea of what you can expect as you begin to work on your show:

Music

Since you're performing a musical, it is important to learn the music during the rehearsal process. Your **music director** will teach the cast all the songs in the show and tell you what to practice at home.

Choreography

Since most musicals include some movement or dance, you'll also be rehearsing choreography. Your **choreographer** will create the dances and teach them to the cast. The music and the choreography help tell the story.

Blocking & Scene Work

Your director will determine where everyone in the cast stands and how they move around the stage. You'll use theater **blocking** terms (downstage left, upstage right, etc.) a lot during this portion of the rehearsal process. You will also practice speaking your lines and work on memorizing them. Rehearsing your part from memory is called being **off-book**. Your director will help you understand the important action in each scene so you can make the best choices for your character's **objective**, or what your character wants.

Marking Your Script

Notating your script can help you to remember important blocking and direction. Below are some tips to keep you on track.

1 Always write your name legibly on your script. Scripts have a way of getting lost or changing hands during rehearsals.

2 Mark your lines and lyrics with a bright-colored highlighter to make your part stand out on the page. This will allow you to look up from your script during rehearsals, since it will be easier to find your place when you look back down.

3 Underline important stage directions, lines, lyrics, and individual words. For example, if your director wants you to stress a word, underline it in your script.

Save time and space by using the following standard abbreviations:

ON: onstage	**OFF:** offstage	**US:** upstage
DS: downstage	**SL:** stage left	**SR:** stage right
CS: center stage	**X:** cross	

4 You may use these abbreviations to modify other instructions (you could write "R hand up" to remind yourself to raise your right hand). You may also combine them in various ways (you could write "XDSR" to remind yourself to cross downstage right).

5 Draw diagrams to help clarify your blocking. For example, if you are instructed to walk in a circle around a bench, you might draw a box to represent the bench, then draw a circle around it with an arrow indicating the direction in which you are supposed to walk.

6 Draw stick figures to help you remember your choreography.

7 Mark your music with large commas to remind yourself where to take breaths while singing.

8 Although you should feel free to mark up your script, be careful it doesn't become so cluttered with notes that you have a hard time finding your lines on the page!

John Bonavita (Sebastian)

SEBASTIAN
Tell me, child. You got trouble in da mind?

ARIEL
Sebastian!

SEBASTIAN
What is all this?

ARIEL
Um... just a few knick-knacks I've collected, that's all.

SEBASTIAN
You ought to be ashamed of yourself! If your poor father knew about this place, he'd—

ARIEL
You're not gonna tell him, are you? Oh, please, Sebastian! He'd never understand!

SEBASTIAN
Ariel, down <u>here</u> is your home! The human world – it's a mess.

(<u>#13 – UNDER THE SEA</u>.)

XDSR

Under the Sea

SEBASTIAN: Life under the sea is better than anything they got up there...

Buoyant Calypso beat

SEBASTIAN:

The sea - weed is

al - ways green - er   in some-bod - y else - 's lake.

Look toward Ariel

You dream   a - bout   go - ing   up   there,

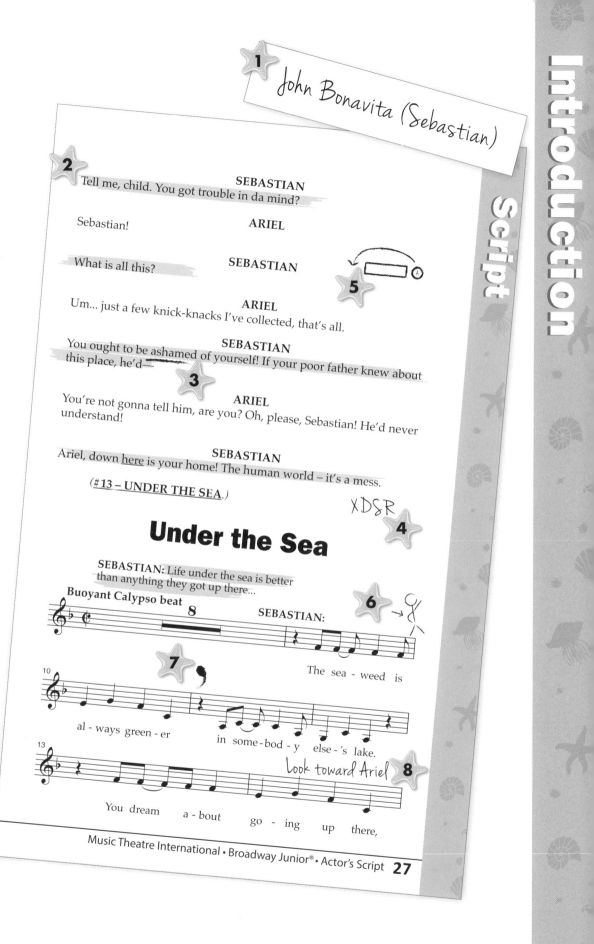

Synopsis

Out on the open sea, **PRINCE ERIC** pursues a mysterious voice despite the protests of his valet, **GRIMSBY** (*Fathoms Below*). Meanwhile, far beneath the waves, the crab **SEBASTIAN** has prepared a concert for **KING TRITON** that will debut his youngest child (*Daughters of Triton*). However, **ARIEL** has gone with her best friend, **FLOUNDER**, to the surface, where they learn about treasures of the world above from the seagull **SCUTTLE** (*Human Stuff*). Deep within her lair, the sea witch **URSULA** and her lackey eels, **FLOTSAM** and **JETSAM**, bemoan their exile and plot to regain power from King Triton using Ariel as bait.

At court, King Triton scolds Ariel for going to the surface and appoints Sebastian as her chaperone. Ariel retreats to her grotto and dreams of living on land (*Part of Your World*). Upon discovering her collection of human objects, Sebastian extols the virtues of ocean life (*Under the Sea*). In the midst of this revelry, Ariel pursues a passing ship until she encounters Prince Eric. Lightning strikes the ship, sending him overboard (*The Storm*). Ariel saves Prince Eric from drowning, brings him safely to shore (*Part of Your World – Reprise*), then disappears into the waves.

Back underwater, the **MERSISTERS** grill Flounder about Ariel's odd behavior (*She's in Love*). When King Triton learns of Ariel's contact with a human, he destroys her grotto. Flotsam and Jetsam find Ariel in despair and lure her to the sea witch's lair. Ursula offers to change Ariel into a human in exchange for her voice (*Poor Unfortunate Souls*). However, Prince Eric must kiss Ariel within three days or she will turn back into a mermaid and become Ursula's slave forever. Overcome by her dreams of the world above, Ariel makes the bargain.

On the beach the next morning, Prince Eric finds the mute Ariel and brings her home to the palace. Sebastian follows to protect Ariel but lands himself in jeopardy in the kitchen of **CHEF LOUIS** (*Les Poissons*). Ariel's silence prompts Prince Eric to find other ways to communicate, like dancing (*One Step Closer*), but he is still determined to find the mysterious voice. On the second day, Sebastian and the **LAGOON ANIMALS** serenade the couple (*Kiss the Girl*), but Flotsam and Jetsam cause a commotion that blocks their kiss. Grimsby arranges a singing contest on the third day to locate the owner of the mysterious voice and thus a bride for Prince Eric (*The Contest*). When Ariel breaks through the crowd and dances for Prince Eric, he realizes how much he loves her and begins to propose. However, Ursula barges in as the sun sets and the spell is broken, turning Ariel back into a mermaid and drawing her into the sea.

Sebastian rushes to warn King Triton, who agrees to hand over his trident and take Ariel's place as Ursula's slave (*Poor Unfortuate Souls – Reprise*). When Prince Eric attempts to rescue Ariel, Ursula loses control of her magic shell, and Ariel's voice is restored. Trident in hand, Ursula attempts to harness the power of the seas but creates a whirlpool that destroys her and the eels. With peace restored, Ariel returns the trident to her father. King Triton realizes how much Ariel cares for Prince Eric and restores her human form. He delivers her to the world above, where Prince Eric rushes up and proposes. As Ariel answers, Prince Eric realizes that it has been her voice all along (*Part of Your World – Finale*).

Theater Tips

- It takes an ensemble to make a show; everyone's part is important.
- Be respectful of others at all times.
- Bring your script and a pencil to every rehearsal.
- Arrive at rehearsal on time and ready to begin.
- Be specific! Make clear choices about your character's background and motivation for each line and action.
- To help memorize your lines, write them down or speak them aloud to yourself in a mirror.
- Don't upstage yourself. **Cheat out** so the audience can always see your face and hear your voice.
- Before each performance, tell everyone to "break a leg" – which is theater talk for "good luck"!
- Be quiet backstage and remember: if you can see the audience, they can see you – so stay out of sight.
- If you forget a line or something unexpected happens onstage, keep going! When you remain confident and in character, it's unlikely that the audience will notice anything is wrong.
- Remember to thank your director and fellow cast and crew.
- **Have fun!**

Characters
(in order of appearance)

SEA CHORUS – storytelling inhabitants of the sea

PILOT – driver of Prince Eric's ship

SAILORS – crew of Prince Eric's ship

PRINCE ERIC – a prince who would rather explore the ocean than govern a kingdom

GRIMSBY – Prince Eric's valet

MERFOLK and **SEA CREATURES** – residents of King Triton's kingdom

SEAHORSE – herald in King Triton's court

KING TRITON – the King of the Sea and Ariel's father

SEBASTIAN – an anxious crab and court composer for King Triton

MERSISTERS (**AQUATA**, **ANDRINA**, **ARISTA**, **ATINA**, **ADELLA**, **ALLANA**) – the daughters of King Triton and Ariel's sisters

ARIEL – King Triton's youngest daughter who longs to be human

FLOUNDER – a rambunctious young fish and Ariel's best friend

SCUTTLE – a zany seagull and self-proclaimed expert on humans

GULLS – Scuttle's friends and fellow seagulls

URSULA – a Sea Witch with a vendetta

TENTACLES – extensions of Ursula, perhaps poor unfortunate souls

FLOTSAM and **JETSAM** – electric eels and Ursula's lackeys

CARLOTTA – headmistress in Prince Eric's palace

CHEF LOUIS – head chef in Prince Eric's palace

CHEFS – Chef Louis's assistants

LAGOON ANIMALS – musical inhabitants of Prince Eric's lagoon

PRINCESSES – neighboring royalty, vying for Prince Eric's hand in marriage

SCENE ONE: THE OCEAN SURFACE

*(#1 – **ORCHESTRA TUNE-UP** starts the show. #2 – **FATHOMS BELOW** immediately follows. The SEA CHORUS enters and creates the surface of the ocean. A ship appears with the PILOT at the wheel and SAILORS at work on deck.)*

Fathoms Below

Boisterious Sea Shanty

sail - or be - ware, 'cause a big - un's a - brew-in'...

...Mys -

I'll

ter - i-ous fath-oms be - low! Heave ho!

sing you a song of the King of the Sea...

...an' it's

The

hey to the star - board, heave ho!_____

ru - ler of all of the o - ceans is he...

...in mys -

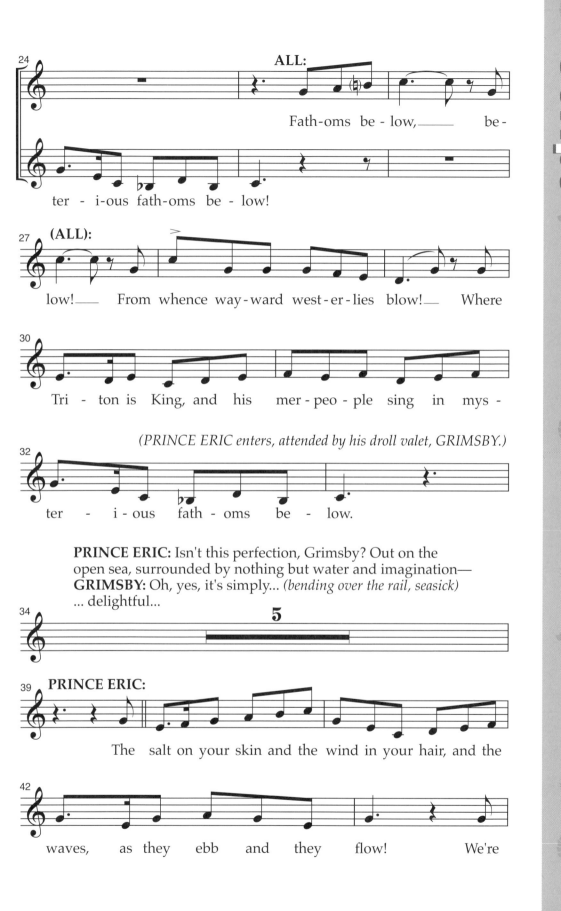

24 ALL:
Fath-oms be-low,____ be-

ter - i-ous fath-oms be - low!

27 (ALL):
low!____ From whence way-ward west-er-lies blow!____ Where

30
Tri - ton is King, and his mer-peo-ple sing in mys-

(PRINCE ERIC enters, attended by his droll valet, GRIMSBY.)

32
ter - i - ous fath - oms be - low.

PRINCE ERIC: Isn't this perfection, Grimsby? Out on the open sea, surrounded by nothing but water and imagination— **GRIMSBY:** Oh, yes, it's simply... *(bending over the rail, seasick)* ... delightful...

34
5

39 **PRINCE ERIC:**
The salt on your skin and the wind in your hair, and the

42
waves, as they ebb and they flow! We're

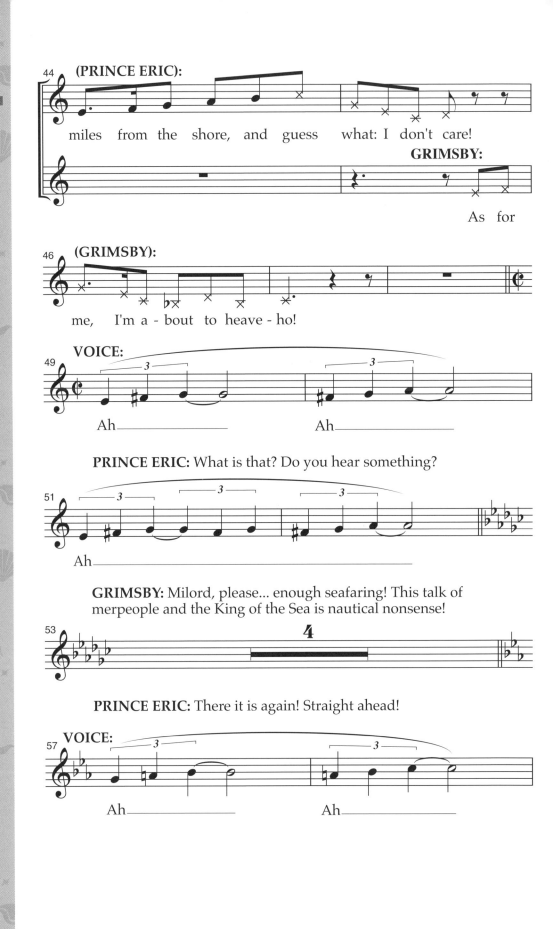

(PRINCE ERIC):

miles from the shore, and guess what: I don't care!

GRIMSBY:

As for

(GRIMSBY):

me, I'm a - bout to heave - ho!

VOICE:

Ah_____ Ah_____

PRINCE ERIC: What is that? Do you hear something?

Ah_____

GRIMSBY: Milord, please... enough seafaring! This talk of merpeople and the King of the Sea is nautical nonsense!

PRINCE ERIC: There it is again! Straight ahead!

VOICE:

Ah_____ Ah_____

GRIMSBY: Your Majesty, you've got to return to court and take up your father's crown!

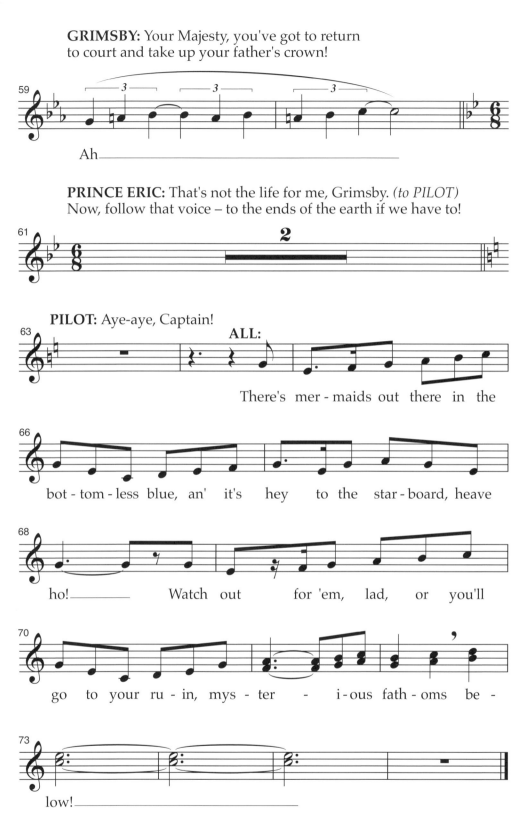

Ah

PRINCE ERIC: That's not the life for me, Grimsby. *(to PILOT)* Now, follow that voice – to the ends of the earth if we have to!

PILOT: Aye-aye, Captain!

ALL:

There's mer - maids out there in the bot - tom - less blue, an' it's hey to the star - board, heave ho! Watch out for 'em, lad, or you'll go to your ru - in, mys - ter - i-ous fath - oms be - low!

*(The "ship" dissolves as ALL exit on #3 – **TRITON'S COURT**.)*

SCENE TWO: KING TRITON'S COURT

(The SEA CHORUS "descends" below the surface to create an elegant undersea court. MERFOLK and SEA CREATURES gather around KING TRITON, who holds his mighty trident.)

KING TRITON

Benevolent merfolk... welcome! It's wonderful to see all of you here.
> *(beat, more serious)*

Ever since the Sea Witch robbed us of your dear Queen, celebrations like these have lifted my spirits. Thank you.

(A SEAHORSE swims forward to make an announcement.)

SEAHORSE

Presenting the Court Composer:

> *(#4 – **SEBASTIAN'S FANFARE**. The crab SEBASTIAN enters.)*

Horatio Thelonius Ignatius Crustaceous Sebastian!

SEBASTIAN

Oh, Sire! You're gonna love this number! I wrote it for my star pupil—

KING TRITON

And who might that be?

SEBASTIAN

Your youngest! Such a voice, that child! Notes as clear as ice, pitch as pure as water! Why, I haven't heard such magnificent sound since the Queen...

KING TRITON

May she rest in peace.

SEBASTIAN

Oh, you're gonna be so proud!
> *(under his breath)*

If only that girl would show up for rehearsals once in a while...

KING TRITON

Well, what are we waiting for? Let the festivities begin!

> *(#5 – **DAUGHTERS OF TRITON**. The MERSISTERS enter and assemble to sing.)*

Daughters of Triton

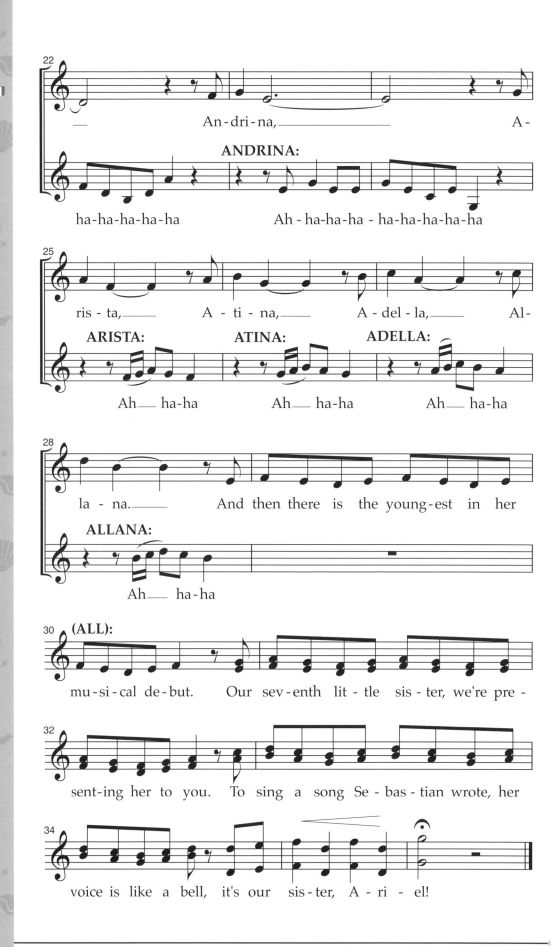

(The MERSISTERS have reassembled to pave the way for ARIEL's entrance. But there's no ARIEL. SEBASTIAN clears his throat and conducts another try. #6 – WHERE'S ARIEL?)

Where's Ariel?

MERSISTERS:

It's our sis-ter, A-ri-el!

(Still no ARIEL.)

SEBASTIAN
Not again, child. I was counting on you most of all!

KING TRITON
Ariel! Where in the name of Poseidon is that girl?

(#7 – THE BEACH. The MERSISTERS complain as ALL exit, revealing two electric eels, FLOTSAM and JETSAM, who have been spying on the affair. They nod to each other and exit.)

SCENE THREE: THE BEACH

(The SEA CHORUS "ascends" to create the ocean surface near the shore. ARIEL, a beautiful young mermaid, enters with a splash. Another splash nearby reveals FLOUNDER, a rambunctious young fish and Ariel's best friend.)

FLOUNDER
Hey, Ariel! There you are!

ARIEL
Just look, Flounder! The sun, the sand... isn't it the most beautiful place you've ever seen?

FLOUNDER
I dunno, Ariel... I'm not sure we ought to be up here.

ARIEL
Don't be such a guppy!

FLOUNDER

A guppy?!? I'm as brave as you are! I'm not afraid of anything—

ARIEL

What about sharks?

FLOUNDER

Where?!?

ARIEL

Oh, Flounder, you really are a guppy!

FLOUNDER

I am not!

ARIEL

Awww...
(gives FLOUNDER an affectionate pat on the head)
You'll never guess what I found today. Look!
(lifts up a large silver serving fork)
Have you ever seen anything so wonderful in your entire life?

FLOUNDER

Wow! Cool! What is it?

ARIEL

I don't know... but I bet Scuttle will! Come on, I'll race you!

(#8 – **FINDING SCUTTLE**. With a splash, ARIEL hits the water.)

FLOUNDER

Hey, wait for me!

(The SEA CHORUS moves to create the effect of ARIEL and
FLOUNDER swimming through the water. The SEA CHORUS
forms a small rock island. SCUTTLE, a seagull, enters, humming
and looking through the wrong end of a telescope.)

ARIEL
(surfaces and swims right up to SCUTTLE)
Scuttle!

SCUTTLE
(calling out to ARIEL "in the distance")
Mermaid off the port bow! Ariel, how you doin', kid?
(puts down the telescope and sees ARIEL up close)
Whoa! What a swim!

ARIEL

(waving the fork)

Scuttle, look what we found!

SCUTTLE

More human stuff, eh? Lemme see...

FLOUNDER

Can you tell us what it's for?

SCUTTLE

Wow! This is special. This is very, very... unusual.

ARIEL

What? What is it?

SCUTTLE

It's a dinglehopper!

ARIEL

A dinglehopper?

SCUTTLE

Oh, these babies are fantabulous... absolutely indispensary.

(**#9 – HUMAN STUFF**.)

Human Stuff

SCUTTLE: When it comes to dinglehoppers,
I'm a regular encyclopoodia!

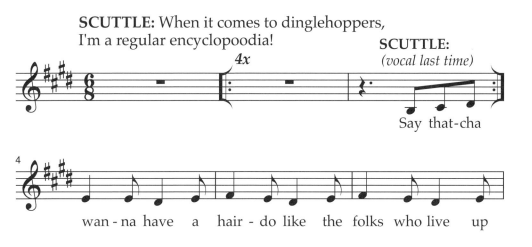

SCUTTLE:
(vocal last time)

Say that-cha

wan - na have a hair - do like the folks who live up

(SCUTTLE): just like so. Twirl it the way I'm twirl - ing now... Give it a lit - tle yank, and there ya go! You're what they call "the dog's me - ow"!

SCUTTLE, GULLS: Won-der-ful stuff!

GULL 3: Awwwk! SCUTTLE, GULLS: That hu - man stuff! Can't get e -

nough... GULL 3: Awwwk! SCUTTLE, GULLS: ...of hu - man stuff! And

we are the au-thor-i-ty, no need for us to bluff! Be-

cause we're great at ex-pla-na-tin' hu - man stuff!

(SCUTTLE pulls out a pipe.)
ARIEL: What's that?
SCUTTLE: A snarfblatt!
ARIEL: Wow!

4

SCUTTLE:

When they in-ven-ted snarf-blatts, just by chance,

sud-den-ly life was la - di - da!

Snarf-blatts are what you use___ to make folks dance!

Give it a blow, and then... *voi - là!*

SCUTTLE,
GULLS:

Won-der - ful stuff!

SCUTTLE,
GULL 3: GULLS:

Awwwk! That hu - man stuff! If you're a

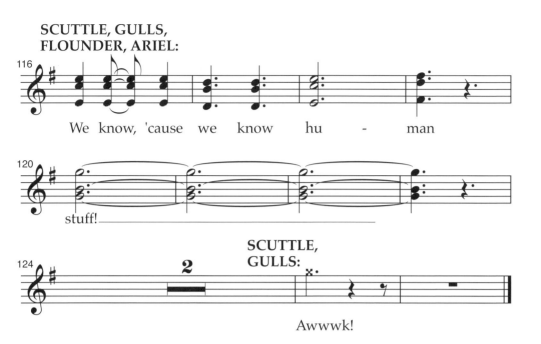

SCUTTLE, GULLS, FLOUNDER, ARIEL:

We know, 'cause we know hu - man stuff!

SCUTTLE, GULLS:

Awwwk!

FLOUNDER
(with pipe in mouth)
Does this thing really work?

SCUTTLE
(takes the pipe from FLOUNDER)
Sure thing, kid, and I ain't just blowin' smoke. It makes music the likes of which you never heard—

ARIEL
Music? Oh no! The concert! My father's gonna kill me!

FLOUNDER
The concert was today?

ARIEL
I completely forgot! Come on, Flounder. Thank you, Scuttle!

SCUTTLE
Anytime, sweets. Anytime!

(**#10 – HUMAN STUFF – PLAYOFF / INTO URSULA'S LAIR**. *ARIEL and FLOUNDER dive underwater. SCUTTLE and the GULLS flap away.*)

SCENE FOUR: URSULA'S LAIR

(We catch up with FLOTSAM and JETSAM as the SEA CHORUS descends and reconfigures to form the dark and sinister lair of the Sea Witch. The EELS are ssso ssslippery that they even ssslither their ssspeech.)

JETSAM

Oh, Sssorceress of the Ssssea!

FLOTSAM

Oh, Beauty of the Brine!

JETSAM, FLOTSAM

Hail to the Sssea Witch! Hail to Ursssula!

(URSULA the Sea Witch enters with her TENTACLES stretching out in all directions. A magic shell sparkles and glows as it hangs from a chain around her neck.)

URSULA

Flotsam, my pet! Jetsam, my darling! Come to me, my little seaspies!

(As Ursula's TENTACLES wrap around the EELS, they sizzle with electricity.)

Mama's feeling... woebegone – banished to the nether regions of the sea. No food, hardly any company... I'm simply wasting away!

JETSAM, FLOTSAM

Poor Ursssssula!

URSULA

Yes, poor me! What news do you have?

FLOTSAM

King Triton and the merfolk are celebrating your defeat!

JETSAM

And he blames you for the queen's demise...

URSULA

Of course he does!
(strokes the magic shell)
Use a little black magic to help out a few merfolk, and this is the thanks I get! Well, now it's time to turn the tides on Triton. We just need to find his Achilles heel... a weakness that will crack his armor...

(URSULA, TENTACLES, and EELS pulsate as they think. Then, the EELS get an idea!)

FLOTSAM

The King is terribly devoted to his daughtersss...

JETSAM

Especially the youngest, with the beautiful voice...

FLOTSAM

But – she misssed the celebration...

URSULA

Hmmm... Apparently Ariel takes her gift for granted... just like her mother did! A woman doesn't know how precious her voice is until she's been silenced.

FLOTSAM, JETSAM

Sssilenced...

URSULA

You two find out what that girl really wants then lure her here to my lair. I'll whip up a little spell to make her dreams come true. Once we have her trapped, Triton will rush to her rescue. And then, my dears...

FLOTSAM, JETSAM

Yesss...?

URSULA, TENTACLES

The trident, crown, and throne will all be mine!!!

(#11 – INTO KING TRITON'S COURT. *URSULA, FLOTSAM, and JETSAM exit in electrical delight.)*

SCENE FIVE: KING TRITON'S COURT

(The SEA CHORUS reconfigures to form the undersea court. KING TRITON enters with SEBASTIAN at his side. ARIEL bursts in, followed by FLOUNDER.)

ARIEL
Daddy, forgive me, I'm so sorry. I just forgot—

KING TRITON
As a result of your careless behavior—

SEBASTIAN
Careless and reckless behavior!

KING TRITON
The entire celebration was—

SEBASTIAN
Ruined! Completely destroyed! This concert was going to be the pinnacle of my distinguished career—

KING TRITON
Sebastian—

ARIEL
But I didn't mean to—

KING TRITON
Ariel, listen. You've been given a gift... your mother's voice. It's a wondrous talent, one that demands stewardship and care. So please, dear child, for the sake of her memory—

ARIEL
I know, Daddy. I know.

FLOUNDER
It wasn't even Ariel's fault! We were gonna come back straight away. But then the seagull started goin' on and on about human stuff—

KING TRITON
Seagull? Human stuff? You went up to the surface?!?

ARIEL
(sheepishly)
Um... nothing happened—

KING TRITON

You could've been seen by one of those barbarians!

ARIEL

Daddy, they're not barbarians!

KING TRITON

They're dangerous – nets, harpoons! You're my youngest—

ARIEL

I'm old enough to look after myself—

KING TRITON

As long as you live under my reef, you'll obey my rules!

ARIEL

If you'd just listen to me for once—

KING TRITON

That's the last time you're ever swimming to the surface! Understood?

ARIEL

You're so unfair!

(ARIEL bursts into tears and swims away, followed by FLOUNDER.)

KING TRITON

Agh! She's stubborn as a barnacle—

SEBASTIAN

Teenagers! Give 'em an inch, and they swim all over you.

KING TRITON

I can govern a kingdom, but I can't control my own daughter. Maybe I was too harsh...

SEBASTIAN

Nonsense, Sire! If you ask me, you haven't been tough enough.

KING TRITON

I haven't?

SEBASTIAN

Ariel needs constant supervision! Someone to watch over her – to keep her out of trouble.

KING TRITON

That's not a bad idea—

SEBASTIAN

I'd say it's a right good one.

KING TRITON

And <u>you</u> are just the crab to do it!

SEBASTIAN

What?!?

KING TRITON

You heard me! From now on, Ariel is <u>your</u> responsibility!

(KING TRITON exits emphatically.)

SEBASTIAN
(follows KING TRITON, pleading)
Mine? But Your Majesty, she's a clever mermaid! I'm just a crustacean!
Surely you ought to pick someone higher on the evolutionary ladder...

SCENE SIX: ARIEL'S GROTTO

*(#12 – PART OF YOUR WORLD. The SEA CHORUS
reconfigures to form Ariel's grotto, filled with "human treasures."
ARIEL, distraught after her fight with Dad, sits among her treasures
holding her newly acquired fork. FLOUNDER floats nearby.)*

Part of Your World

ARIEL: If only I could make my father understand. I just don't see how a world that makes such wonderful things could be so bad.

Look at this stuff.   Is - n't it neat?

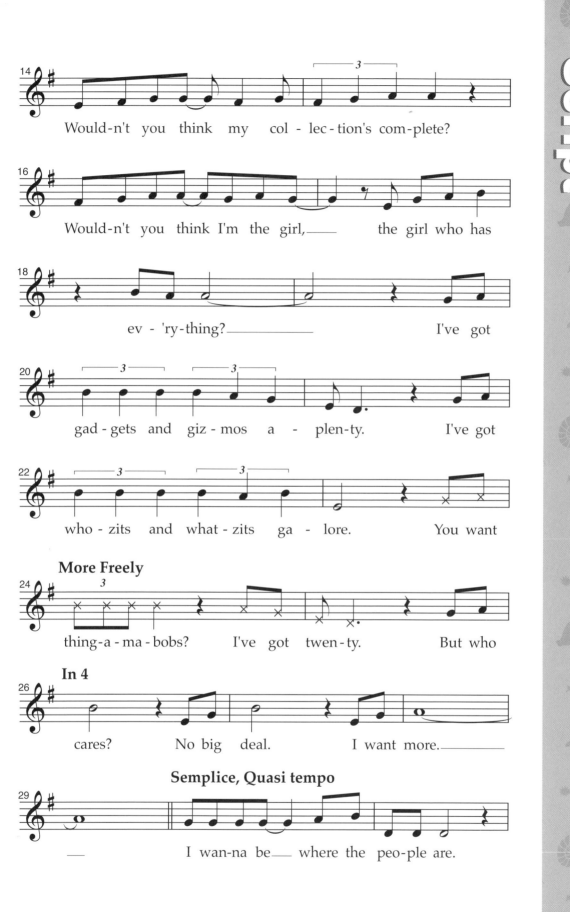

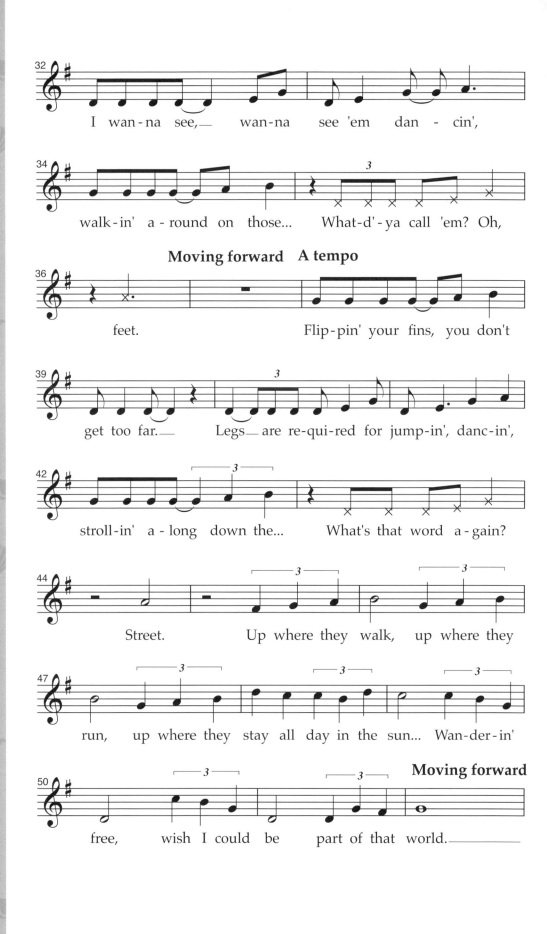

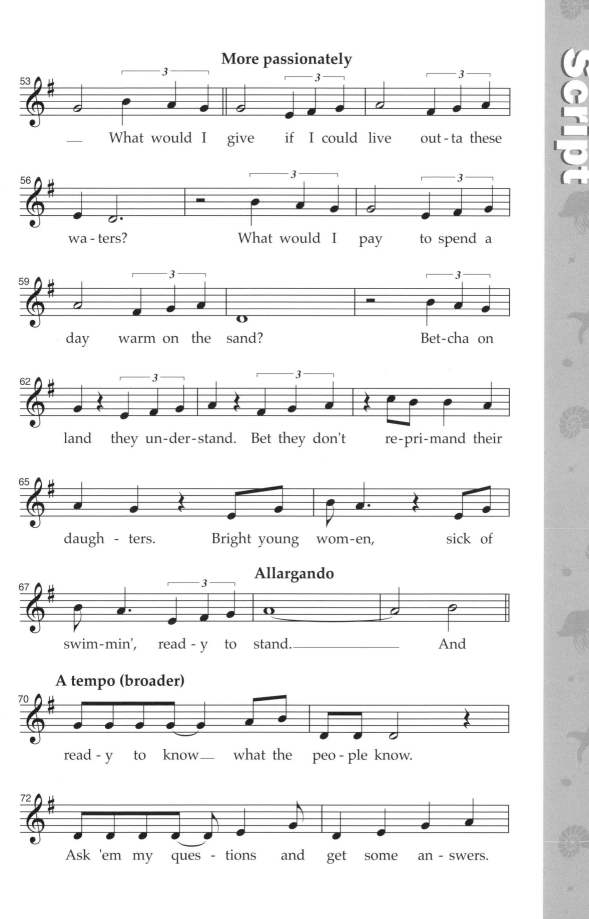

What's a fire?___ And why does it... What's the word?

Burn?___ When's it my turn? Would-n't I

love, love to ex - plore that shore up a - bove?___

Freely

___ Out of the sea, wish I could

A tempo

be part of that world.___

(FLOTSAM and JETSAM, who have been spying, enter unseen. They whisper to each other:)

FLOTSAM

"Sssick of ssswimin'..."?

JETSAM

"Out of the sssea..."?

FLOTSAM, JETSAM

Hmmm...

(As SEBASTIAN enters, FLOTSAM and JETSAM disappear into the shadows.)

SEBASTIAN

Tell me, child. You got trouble in da mind?

ARIEL

Sebastian!

SEBASTIAN

What is all this?

ARIEL

Um... just a few knick-knacks I've collected, that's all.

SEBASTIAN

You ought to be ashamed of yourself! If your poor father knew about this place, he'd—

ARIEL

You're not gonna tell him, are you? Oh, please, Sebastian! He'd never understand!

SEBASTIAN

Ariel, down <u>here</u> is your home! The human world – it's a mess.

(**#13 – UNDER THE SEA**.)

Under the Sea

SEBASTIAN: Life under the sea is better than anything they got up there...

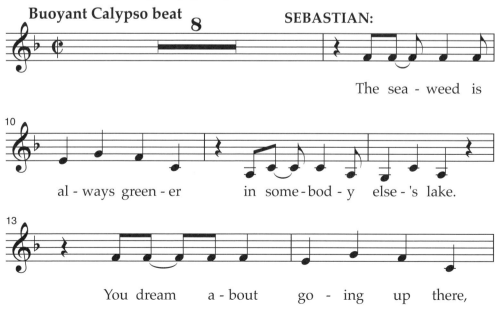

Buoyant Calypso beat

SEBASTIAN:

The sea - weed is al - ways green - er in some-bod - y else - 's lake.

You dream a - bout go - ing up there,

but that is a big mis-take. Just look at the

world a - round you, right here on the o - cean floor.

Such won-der-ful things sur-round you. What more is you

look-in' for? Un - der the sea,

un - der the sea. Dar - lin', it's

bet-ter down where it's wet-ter, take it from me.

Up— on the shore they work all day.—

— Out— in the sun they slave a - way

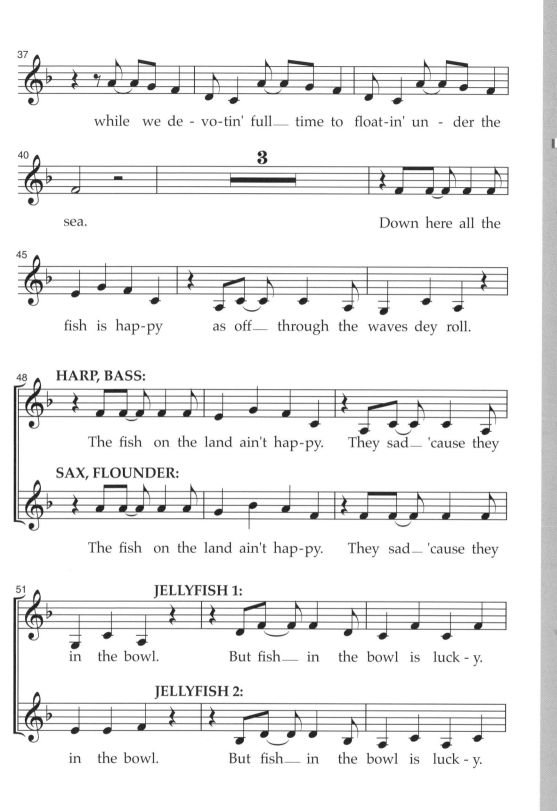

while we de-vo-tin' full___ time to float-in' un-der the

sea.   Down here all the

fish is hap-py   as off___ through the waves dey roll.

HARP, BASS:

The fish on the land ain't hap-py.   They sad___ 'cause they

SAX, FLOUNDER:

The fish on the land ain't hap-py.   They sad___ 'cause they

JELLYFISH 1:

in the bowl.   But fish___ in the bowl is luck-y.

JELLYFISH 2:

in the bowl.   But fish___ in the bowl is luck-y.

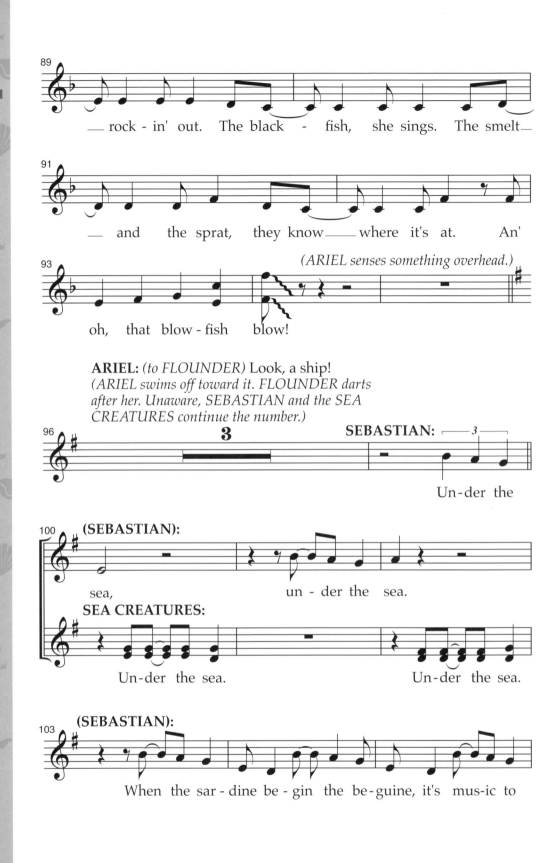

— rock - in' out. The black - fish, she sings. The smelt —

— and the sprat, they know — where it's at. An'

(ARIEL senses something overhead.)

oh, that blow - fish blow!

ARIEL: *(to FLOUNDER)* Look, a ship!
(ARIEL swims off toward it. FLOUNDER darts after her. Unaware, SEBASTIAN and the SEA CREATURES continue the number.)

SEBASTIAN:

Un - der the

(SEBASTIAN):

sea, un - der the sea.

SEA CREATURES:

Un - der the sea. Un - der the sea.

(SEBASTIAN):

When the sar - dine be - gin the be - guine, it's mus - ic to

luck here down in the muck here, un - der the

Un - der, un - der__ the

sea!_____

sea!_____

(The SEA CREATURES exit with **#14 – UNDER THE SEA – PLAYOFF**.*)*

SEBASTIAN

See child, that's what I'm talking about!
> *(looks around to discover ARIEL is missing)*

Ariel! Hello?
> *(exiting)*

Oh, somebody's gotta nail that girl's fins to the floor!

(**#15 – PRINCE ERIC'S SHIP**.*)*

SCENE SEVEN: THE OCEAN SURFACE

Prince Eric's Ship

(The SEA CHORUS "ascends" to form the ocean's surface and the ship from the first scene. PRINCE ERIC enters with GRIMSBY, the PILOT, and SAILORS.)

SAILORS:

Heave ho, Heave ho, Heave ho

(Music continues under dialogue.)

PRINCE ERIC
Now suppose I don't want to be King—

GRIMSBY
I swore an oath to your dear father on his death bed that I'd turn you from a roustabout into a royal and have you married to a princess—

PRINCE ERIC
Ugh!

GRIMSBY
—by your next birthday, which is now just three days away!

PRINCE ERIC
Did you ever try to take a princess sailing? <u>It's a joke!</u> Their dresses get caught in the rigging. And most of 'em can't even swim—

GRIMSBY
You know, there's more to a woman than her flutter kick. Our kingdom needs a <u>queen!</u>

PRINCE ERIC
Where am I gonna find her, Grimsby? A girl who's as carefree and alive as the sea itself. Where?

(ARIEL and FLOUNDER bob up to the surface. SCUTTLE hovers nearby.)

FLOUNDER

(staring up at the ship)

Wow...

(PRINCE ERIC stares out to sea over their heads.)

PRINCE ERIC

It's too much to hope for, isn't it? Somewhere, out there... a girl who's a match for a guy like me?

GRIMSBY

Perhaps you're not looking hard enough.

(ARIEL tries to avoid being seen or heard, but can't help but stare at PRINCE ERIC.)

ARIEL

(whispers)

I've never seen a human this close before.

SCUTTLE

(shouts)

Me neither!

ARIEL

(grabs SCUTTLE's beak)

Shh! I thought you were an expert.

SCUTTLE

(whispers)

On their stuff, sure! But yikes – the sight of 'em! Hideous, ain't it?

ARIEL

I dunno, Scuttle. I think he's really handsome.

PRINCE ERIC

Trust me, Grimsby – when I come across the girl of my dreams, it'll hit me like lightning.

*(With #**16 – THE STORM**, lightning cracks across the sky, along with roaring thunder. The SEA CHORUS creates a storm and rocks the ship. FLOTSAM and JETSAM appear and spy.)*

The Storm

PILOT: Hurricane a'coming, Captain! King Triton must be angry indeed!

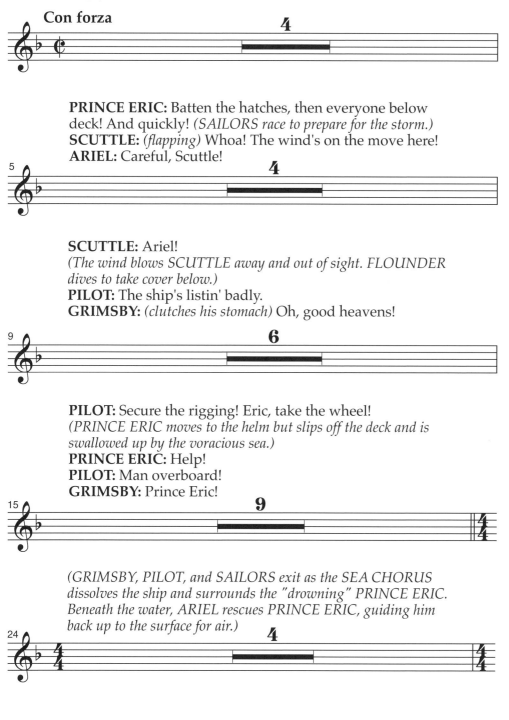

PRINCE ERIC: Batten the hatches, then everyone below deck! And quickly! *(SAILORS race to prepare for the storm.)*
SCUTTLE: *(flapping)* Whoa! The wind's on the move here!
ARIEL: Careful, Scuttle!

SCUTTLE: Ariel!
(The wind blows SCUTTLE away and out of sight. FLOUNDER dives to take cover below.)
PILOT: The ship's listin' badly.
GRIMSBY: *(clutches his stomach)* Oh, good heavens!

PILOT: Secure the rigging! Eric, take the wheel!
(PRINCE ERIC moves to the helm but slips off the deck and is swallowed up by the voracious sea.)
PRINCE ERIC: Help!
PILOT: Man overboard!
GRIMSBY: Prince Eric!

(GRIMSBY, PILOT, and SAILORS exit as the SEA CHORUS dissolves the ship and surrounds the "drowning" PRINCE ERIC. Beneath the water, ARIEL rescues PRINCE ERIC, guiding him back up to the surface for air.)

SEA CHORUS:

p Ah⸻ Ah⸻

Ah⸻

(The SEA CHORUS forms the beach and rock island.)

SCENE EIGHT: THE BEACH

(ARIEL lays PRINCE ERIC safely on the sand. FLOUNDER looks on from the water. SEBASTIAN surfaces nearby, flabbergasted by the scene before him yet too afriad to utter a word or come any closer. FLOTSAM and JETSAM surface further away, unseen. SCUTTLE enters and stands by ARIEL, his feathers mussed from the storm.)

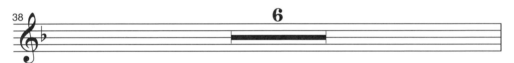

ARIEL: Was I too late?
SCUTTLE: It's hard to say. *(putting his ear against PRINCE ERIC's foot)* Oh, I— I can't make out a heartbeat.

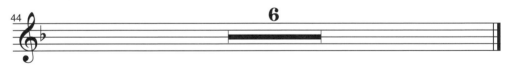

(Suddenly, PRINCE ERIC's chest heaves with life, but he remains semi-conscious.)

ARIEL

No, look!

(#17 – PART OF YOUR WORLD – REPRISE 1.)

Part of Your World
(Reprise 1)

ARIEL: He's breathing! Oh, Scuttle, just look at him. He's so beautiful.

Slowly and expressively ... **Freely**

ARIEL:

What would I give— to live where you are? What would I pay— to stay here, be - side you? What would I do— to see you smil-ing at me...

GRIMSBY

(offstage)
Prince Eric! Ahoy! Somebody! Anybody!

SCUTTLE

On your way, kid... before we's discovered!

(ARIEL slips into the surf, followed by FLOUNDER and SEBASTIAN. Having now seen enough to fuel Ursula's scheme, FLOTSAM and JETSAM also exit. A panicked GRIMSBY enters and sees PRINCE ERIC.)

GRIMSBY

Oh, Prince Eric! Are you all right?

(GRIMSBY)
(to SCUTTLE)
Get away, you filthy bird!

(SCUTTLE squawks and exits, perturbed. GRIMSBY kneels by PRINCE ERIC.)

PRINCE ERIC
(rousing, a little foggy)
A girl rescued me. She pulled me right out of the surf. And she was singing!

GRIMSBY
There, there now. You took a terrible tumble, dear boy—

PRINCE ERIC
That voice! I can't get it out of my head—

(ARIEL resurfaces and perches on the rocks, unseen. GRIMSBY helps PRINCE ERIC to his feet.)

GRIMSBY
Come with me. A night of sleep, and you'll be good as new—

PRINCE ERIC
I must find her! And thank her for saving my life.

GRIMSBY
You've heard too many tall tales, my boy.

PRINCE ERIC
No. She was real.

GRIMSBY
(guiding PRINCE ERIC off)
Yes, Prince Eric. Of course she was. As real as a mermaid on the rocks!

(ARIEL looks after Prince Eric – her crush has a name!
#18 – PART OF YOUR WORLD – REPRISE 2.*)*

Part of Your World
(Reprise 2)

ARIEL: Prince Eric...

I don't know when, I don't know how, but I know some - thing's start - ing right now. Watch and you'll see, some-day I'll be part of your world!

(ARIEL dives into the sea.)

SCENE NINE: KING TRITON'S COURT

*(#19 – **SHE'S IN LOVE**. The SEA CHORUS "descends" and forms the court. The MERSISTERS enter, gossiping.)*

She's in Love

ALLANA: I'm talking about Ariel, that's who!
ADELLA: What about her?
ALLANA: She sure is acting fishy lately!
AQUATA: I'll say! Swimmin' in cirlces! Chasing her tail!
ALLANA: That girl is up to her gills in something!

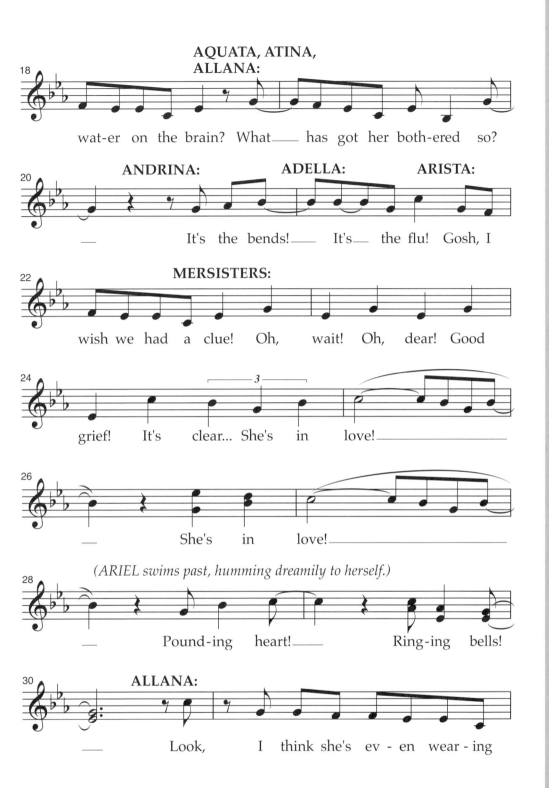

AQUATA, ATINA, ALLANA:
wat-er on the brain? What has got her both-ered so?

ANDRINA: It's the bends! **ADELLA:** It's the flu! **ARISTA:** Gosh, I

MERSISTERS:
wish we had a clue! Oh, wait! Oh, dear! Good

grief! It's clear... She's in love!

She's in love!

(ARIEL swims past, humming dreamily to herself.)

Pound-ing heart! Ring-ing bells!

ALLANA:
Look, I think she's ev - en wear - ing

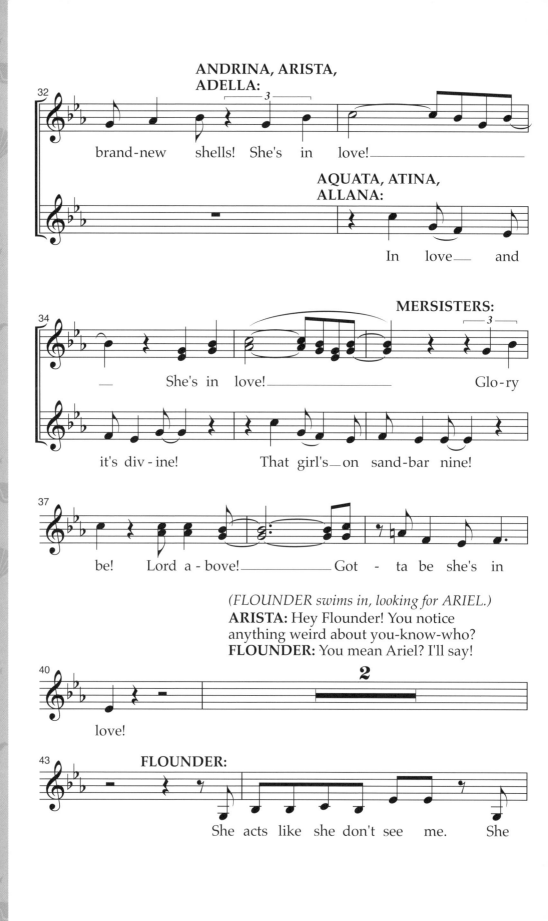

ANDRINA, ARISTA, ADELLA:

brand-new shells! She's in love!

AQUATA, ATINA, ALLANA:

In love___ and

MERSISTERS:

She's in love!___ Glo-ry

it's div-ine! That girl's___on sand-bar nine!

be! Lord a-bove!___ Got - ta be she's in

(FLOUNDER *swims in, looking for ARIEL.*)
ARISTA: Hey Flounder! You notice anything weird about you-know-who?
FLOUNDER: You mean Ariel? I'll say!

love!

FLOUNDER:

She acts like she don't see me. She

doesn't ev-en speak. She treats me like sa-shi-mi left ov-

-er from last week. You see her late at night, tos-

(FLOUNDER):

-sin' in her o-cean bed.——

MERSISTERS:

Shoop, shoop

And she sighs,—— and she swoons, and she's

Shoop, shoop

(FLOUNDER): ⌐**MERSISTERS:**

hum-min' lit-tle tunes... Ev - en has a sort of glow.

FLOUNDER:

— What on earth—— could it be?——

MERSISTERS:

A - ny

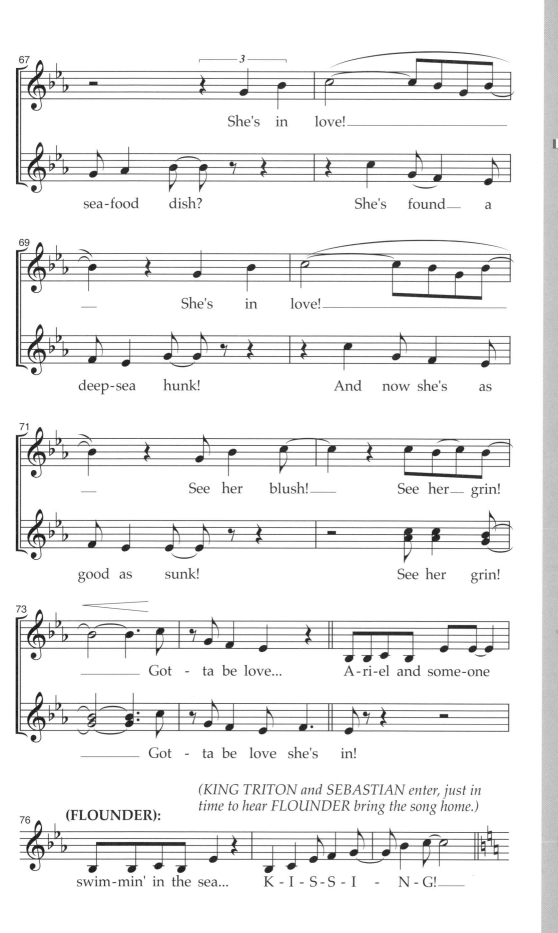

She's in love!

sea-food dish? She's found a

She's in love!

deep-sea hunk! And now she's as

See her blush! See her grin!

good as sunk! See her grin!

Got - ta be love... A - ri-el and some-one

Got - ta be love she's in!

(KING TRITON and SEBASTIAN enter, just in time to hear FLOUNDER bring the song home.)

(FLOUNDER):

swim-min' in the sea... K - I - S - S - I - N - G!

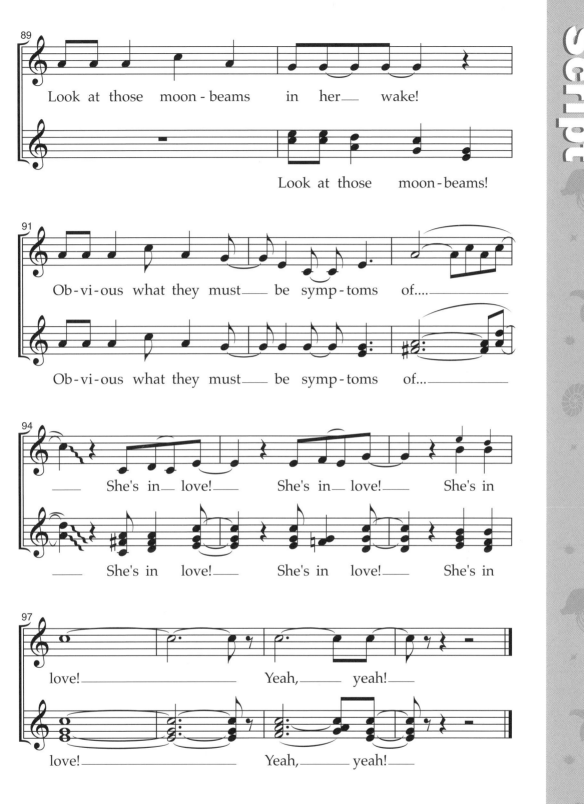

Look at those moon-beams in her — wake!

Look at those moon-beams!

Ob-vi-ous what they must — be symp-toms of....

Ob-vi-ous what they must — be symp-toms of...

— She's in — love! — She's in — love! — She's in

— She's in — love! — She's in — love! — She's in

love! — Yeah, — yeah! —

love! — Yeah, — yeah! —

(#20 – FLOUNDER FLOUNDERS.)

KING TRITON

In love – my little Ariel? So <u>that</u> explains it!

(FLOUNDER tries to swim away inconspicuously.)

(KING TRITON)

Just a minute there, Flounder.

FLOUNDER

Who, me?

KING TRITON

You know Ariel as well as anybody. Who's the lucky merman?

FLOUNDER

Gee, I dunno. I didn't even know it was love until the second chorus!

KING TRITON

Sebastian? Any ideas?

SEBASTIAN

I've tried to stop her, Sire, but she doesn't listen! I tell her, "Ariel, you've got to stay away from those humans – they're nothing but trouble—"

(FLOUNDER bolts.)

KING TRITON

Humans? What about humans?

SEBASTIAN

Who said anything about humans?

(SEBASTIAN scampers off.)

KING TRITON
(pursuing SEBASTIAN)

Sebastian, have you been keeping secrets from me? Where is that girl?!?

SCENE TEN: ARIEL'S GROTTO

(#21 – ARIEL'S GROTTO. The SEA CHORUS "follows" KING TRITON to Ariel's grotto. ARIEL enters, examining a telescope that she recovered after the storm.)

ARIEL

And now let me see... what did Scuttle call this one? Is it a ditty-whumper? A thumb-doodle? Whatever it is... Prince Eric held it in his own strong, beautiful human hands—

(An enraged KING TRITON bursts in.)

KING TRITON

Ariel!
> *(taken aback by the collection of human stuff)*

What is all this?!?

ARIEL

Daddy, they're my—

KING TRITON

Human junk!

ARIEL

No, treasures!

KING TRITON

Did you save a human from drowning?

ARIEL

He would've died!

KING TRITON

That savage brute could have killed you! And it's my job to keep you safe from harm.

ARIEL

But he didn't frighten me. He made me feel... wonderful! Besides, I am not a child anymore!

KING TRITON

No? Well, you are certainly talking like one. He's a <u>human</u> – you're a <u>mermaid</u>.

ARIEL

It doesn't matter – you don't understand! I wish mother were here!

KING TRITON
> *(takes a moment to recover from the low blow)*

Ariel, I miss your mother just as much as you do. But I am still the King. And you are not to go to the surface ever again. Am I clear?!?

> *(Now losing his temper, KING TRITON takes the telescope from her and crushes it. He then raises his trident to destroy the other treasures in the grotto. #22 – **GROTTO DESTRUCTION**. The SEA CHORUS reels from the trident's three powerful blasts. ARIEL bursts into tears then falls into a distraught mermaid heap. KING TRITON starts to swim off. SEBASTIAN enters to see the destruction. KING TRITON pauses for a moment of regret.)*

(KING TRITON)
I'm just trying to protect her, Sebastian.

SEBASTIAN
She'll be all right, Sire. Just give her some time.

(KING TRITON exits. SEBASTIAN gingerly approaches ARIEL.)

ARIEL
I <u>hate</u> him!

SEBASTIAN
Ariel, don't say—

ARIEL
And some friend you turned out to be – spilling everything—

SEBASTIAN
I couldn't help it! He had my claws in a clamp!

ARIEL
I don't need you. I don't need any of you! Go away!
(SEBASTIAN drops his head.)
I said, <u>go away</u>!
(SEBASTIAN exits. ARIEL sobs.)
I don't belong here. If only I could be up there...

(FLOTSAM and JETSAM, who have been ssspying, as usual, ssslither in and approach ARIEL.)

JETSAM
Poor, sssweet, misssunderstood child.

FLOTSAM
She has a very ssserious problem, hasn't she?

JETSAM
Who will ease her woes and worries?

FLOTSAM
Who will help her get her man?

(FLOTSAM and JETSAM circle a startled ARIEL.)

JETSAM, FLOTSAM
Perhaps the Sea Witch can!

ARIEL

Who are – how did you—

JETSAM

She's been dying to help you!

ARIEL

Ursula? Help <u>me</u>?

FLOTSAM

Oh, yesss... but she can't leave her lair...

ARIEL

(weighs fear against desire... then relents:)
Then take me to her!

FLOTSAM, JETSAM

Of courssse...!

*(#23 – **MURKY WATERS**. FLOTSAM and JETSAM usher
ARIEL into the darkness. Suddenly, FLOUNDER appears.)*

FLOUNDER

Hello? Ariel! Where'd you go?
(sees ARIEL swim away with FLOTSAM and JETSAM)
Oh, no!
(swims off in a panic)
Sebastian!

SCENE ELEVEN: URSULA'S LAIR

*(The SEA CHORUS shifts to form Ursula's lair. FLOTSAM and
JETSAM enter with ARIEL, who is having second thoughts.)*

FLOTSAM

Oh, Mistress of the Deep! You've a visitor...

ARIEL

(turns to leave)
I don't know if—

JETSAM

(blocking ARIEL's way out)
Now, now...

FLOTSAM

Mustn't get cold fins!

(URSULA appears. Her TENTACLES reach out toward ARIEL, who stiffens in fear.)

URSULA

Don't be shy, Ariel darling!

ARIEL

I – I shouldn't be here. Mother died because of you.

URSULA

Oh child... what happened to your dear mother was a terrible, unfortunate <u>accident</u> – poor soul.

ARIEL

An... accident?

URSULA

Of course! I did my very best to <u>save</u> her.

ARIEL

You did? But Father told me—

URSULA

The <u>truth</u> is that the ocean wasn't big enough for both your father and me, so he sent me here. And now I see he's driven you away, too...

ARIEL

He doesn't understand me.

URSULA

Oh, but I do, dumpling. We're so very alike, you and I – gals with ambition! Now tell me absolutely everything.

(FLOTSAM and JETSAM swim next to URSULA, who pets them for a job well done. With the entrance unguarded, FLOUNDER and SEBASTIAN peek in and observe, unnoticed.)

ARIEL

I'm in love with someone. A human.

URSULA

A prince, I hear. Quite a catch! Well, the answer is simple: You've got to become human yourself!

ARIEL

Can you do that?

URSULA

My dear, sweet child – it's what I live for: to help unfortunate merfolk like yourself.

(#24 – POOR UNFORTUNATE SOULS.)

Poor Unfortunate Souls

**Moderate 2 -
1930s Cabaret Feel**

URSULA: Poor souls with no one else to turn to...

URSULA:
I ad - mit that in the past I've been a

nas-ty. They were-n't kid-ding when they called me, well, a

witch. But you'll find that now - a - days, I've

mend - ed all my ways, re - pent-ed, seen the light, and made a

A tempo

switch. True? Yes. And I for - tu - nate-ly know a lit - tle

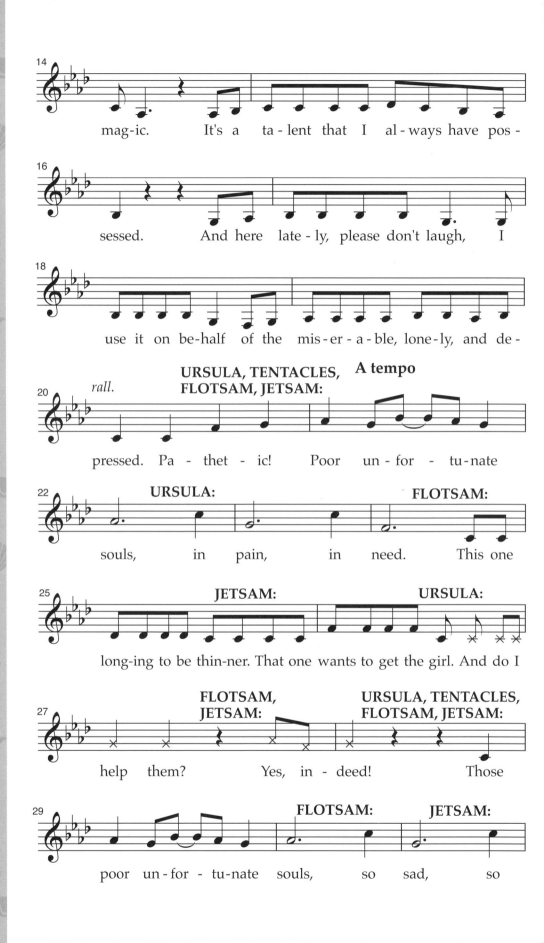

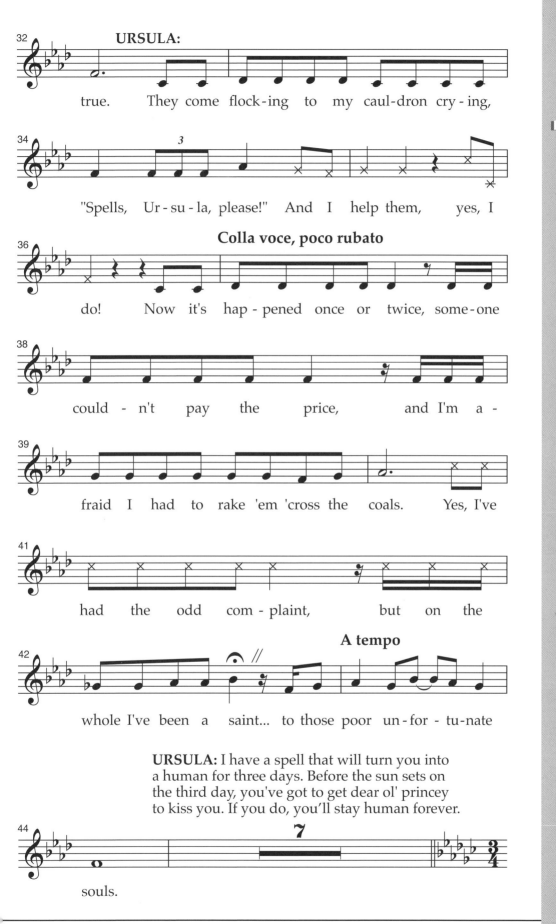

32 URSULA:

true. They come flock-ing to my caul-dron cry-ing,

34 3

"Spells, Ur-su-la, please!" And I help them, yes, I

Colla voce, poco rubato

36

do! Now it's hap-pened once or twice, some-one

38

could-n't pay the price, and I'm a-

39

fraid I had to rake 'em 'cross the coals. Yes, I've

41

had the odd com-plaint, but on the

A tempo

42

whole I've been a saint... to those poor un-for-tu-nate

URSULA: I have a spell that will turn you into a human for three days. Before the sun sets on the third day, you've got to get dear ol' princey to kiss you. If you do, you'll stay human forever.

44 **7**

souls.

ARIEL: And if I don't?

URSULA: You will turn back into a mermaid and your soul will be mine forever! *(ARIEL gasps.)* Life's full of tough choices, isn't it?

(URSULA): Of course, there is one more thing... my fee.

ARIEL: But I don't have any—

URSULA: I'm not asking for much. Only... your voice.

ARIEL: But if I give away my voice, how can I ever—

URSULA:

Tempo 1°, poco piu mosso

You'll have your looks... Your pret-ty face... And don't un-der-es-ti-mate the im-por-tance... of bo-dy lan-guage!

A tempo

Come on, you poor un-for-tu-nate soul! Go a-head! Make your choice! I'm a ver-y bus-y wom-an and I

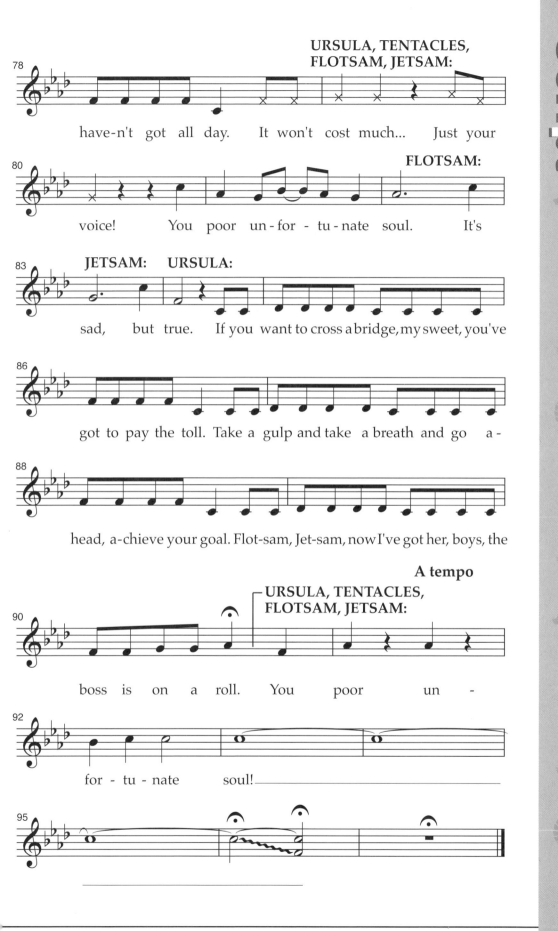

URSULA

So how's about it, cupcake?

ARIEL
(the highest stakes before her)
If I become human, will I ever see my family again?

(#25 – BELUGA SEVRUGA.)

Beluga Sevruga

(ARIEL): My sisters... Daddy—
URSULA: Now do you want princey-poo or not?
(rapid countdown) Five, four, three, two—
ARIEL: Yes! Yes, I'll do it!

Very slowly, rubato

5

URSULA:
That a girl! Now...

Forcefully, poco rubato

URSULA:

Be - lu-ga, Se-vru-ga, come

Piu mosso

winds of the Cas-pi-an Sea...___ La -

rynx-es, gla - cy - dis, ad max la-ryn-gi-tis, la

URSULA: Now, sing!
Sing your voice over to me!
*(URSULA holds out the
magic shell toward ARIEL.)*

vo - ce to me!___

Moderato

ARIEL:

Ah_____ Ah_____ Ah_____

URSULA: Sing and keep singing!

Ah_____ Ah_____ Ah_____

Ah_____ Ah_____ Ah_____

(As ARIEL's voice soars, URSULA traps it in her shell.)
URSULA: Now swim, swim, swim for your life, human child!
*(URSULA, the TENTACLES, FLOTSAM, and JETSAM cackle
with glee as they exit. The SEA CHORUS now becomes open
sea that surrounds ARIEL, who starts to float toward the surface.)*

Forceful and fast

11

*(In a magical spin, ARIEL sheds her tail, revealing human legs.
FLOUNDER and SEBASTIAN swim behind. The SEA CHORUS
forms the beach. As the sun rises, the first day of the spell begins.)*

8

*(ARIEL breaks the surface, takes her first breath with human lungs,
and collapses on the sand.)*

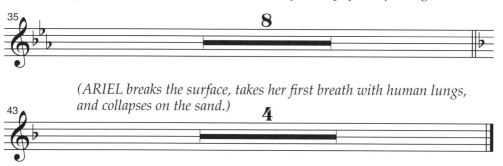

4

(SEBASTIAN and FLOUNDER surface and attend their beloved friend.)

FLOUNDER

Ariel! Are you okay?

SEBASTIAN

Oh child, what have you done?

(After a moment, ARIEL sits up and stares at her new legs in wonderment. Slowly and shakily she tries to stand, sticking her arms out for balance... then falls on her rear. SCUTTLE flaps in.)

SCUTTLE

Well, look who got beached! Hiya, Ariel! Wait – there's something different about'cha. Don't tell me – it's your hairdo, right? You've been using the dinglehopper!
(ARIEL shakes her head "no.")
Nah? Hmm... I can't quite put my foot on it right now—

SEBASTIAN

She's got <u>legs</u>, you idiot!

FLOUNDER

Ariel traded her voice to the Sea Witch to become human!

SCUTTLE

Nah, kid! Not your beautiful pipes!

(ARIEL nods. She opens her mouth, but no sound.)

SEBASTIAN

Ya see? Not a sound! What would her father say? I'll tell ya what her father'd say: He'd say he's gonna kill himself a crab, that's what he'd say!

FLOUNDER

Now she's got three days to make Prince Eric fall in love with her. And to prove it, he's gotta <u>kiss</u> her!

SCUTTLE

The <u>Prince</u>? Well, I'll say!

(PRINCE ERIC bounds onto the beach, ready to go shipboard. Catching sight of ARIEL, he stops abruptly.)

PRINCE ERIC

Hey, what have we got—?
> *(to SCUTTLE)*

Shoo, shoo.

> *(SCUTTLE squawks, flaps, and moves aside. #26 – ERIC ENTERS. PRINCE ERIC looks closely at ARIEL.)*

(PRINCE ERIC)

Miss, are you all right? You— you seem very familiar... Of course! It's you! I've been looking for you everywhere! What's your name?

> *(ARIEL smiles but holds her throat.)*

Sore throat, huh?

> *(ARIEL draws a finger across her throat, sadly.)*

Oh, you don't speak at all? I'm sorry. For a moment, I mistook you for somebody else.

> *(Frustrated, ARIEL tries to pantomime that she's the one!)*

What is it? You're hurt? No, no... You need help...? Well, I've got just the remedy! A warm bath and a hot meal! Come on now... the palace isn't far.

> *(PRINCE ERIC props up ARIEL and leads her toward the palace.)*

FLOUNDER

Way to go, Ariel!

SCUTTLE

That's what I call "reelin' him in"!

SEBASTIAN

> *(mortified)*

Oh, now I've got to follow her!
> *(scampering off after ARIEL and PRINCE ERIC)*

This is gonna get me in real hot water!

SCUTTLE

> *(to audience)*

Can you believe that guy? What a crab!

> *(#27 – PALACE KITCHEN. SCUTTLE exits. FLOUNDER flutters fins and dives into the water.)*

SCENE THIRTEEN: THE PALACE KITCHEN

(The SEA CHORUS now forms the palace kitchen. CHEF LOUIS, a French culinary perfectionist, orders CHEFS about as he prepares dinner.)

CHEF LOUIS

Attention. Attention! *Le menu pour ce soir:* escargot, lobster bisque, tuna tartare, holy mackerel. *Maintenant!*

(**#28 – LES POISSONS**. *SEBASTIAN enters, grumbling to himself.)*

Les Poissons

SEBASTIAN: The things I do for that girl! Over the wall... under the gutter... in through the window... Now, finally, someplace that's <u>safe</u>! *(realizes he's in the middle of the kitchen)* Uh-oh!
(SEBASTIAN hides as CHEF LOUIS approaches.)

Valse Parisienne – Easy One

CHEF LOUIS: Easy

Les pois - sons, les pois - sons, how I love *les pois - sons.* Love to chop and to serve lit - tle fish. First I cut off their heads, then I pull out the bones. Ah *mais oui, ça c'est*

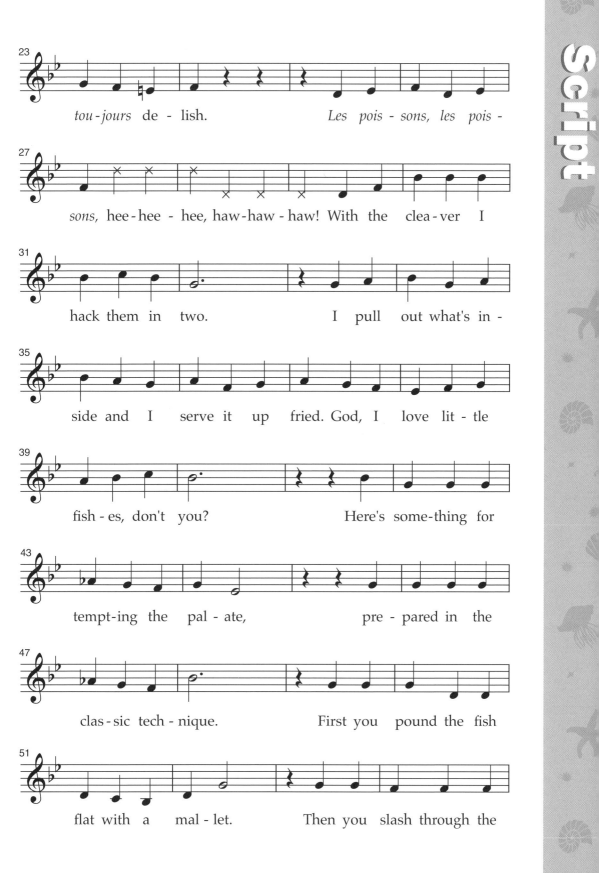

tou - jours de - lish.   *Les pois - sons, les pois -*

sons, hee - hee - hee, haw - haw - haw! With the clea - ver I

hack them in   two.   I   pull   out what's in -

side and   I   serve it   up   fried. God, I   love lit - tle

fish - es, don't   you?   Here's some - thing for

tempt - ing   the   pal - ate,   pre - pared in   the

clas - sic   tech - nique.   First you   pound the fish

flat with   a   mal - let.   Then you   slash through the

skin, give the bel - ly a slice. Then you rub some salt

in... 'cause that makes it taste nice.

Energetic

CHEF LOUIS,
CHEFS:

Les

pois - sons! Les pois - sons! Ooh la

la! Here they are! Say bon - jour to our

friends from the sea! Fish fil -

CHEF 2:   CHEF 3:   CHEF 4:

let! Fish pâ - té! Fish flam - bé! Fish tar -

CHEF LOUIS:

tare! It's a fish... How you say? Jam-bor - ee!

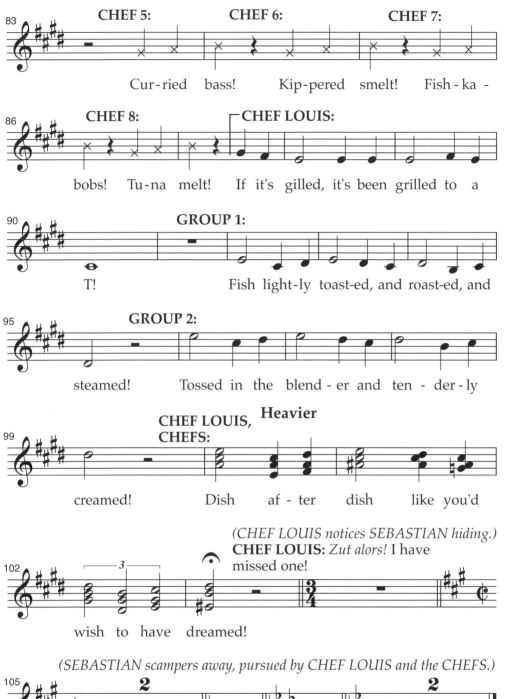

CHEF 5: **CHEF 6:** **CHEF 7:**

Cur-ried bass! Kip-pered smelt! Fish-ka-

CHEF 8: **CHEF LOUIS:**

bobs! Tu-na melt! If it's gilled, it's been grilled to a

GROUP 1:

T! Fish light-ly toast-ed, and roast-ed, and

GROUP 2:

steamed! Tossed in the blend-er and ten-der-ly

CHEF LOUIS, CHEFS: **Heavier**

creamed! Dish af-ter dish like you'd

(CHEF LOUIS notices SEBASTIAN hiding.)
CHEF LOUIS: *Zut alors!* I have
missed one!

wish to have dreamed!

(SEBASTIAN scampers away, pursued by CHEF LOUIS and the CHEFS.)

SCENE FOURTEEN: THE PALACE HALL

(The SEA CHORUS reconfigures to form #29 – THE PALACE HALL. CARLOTTA, the chatty and maternal palace headmistress, enters while fastening ARIEL's new dress.)

CARLOTTA
Imagine, washing up like that on the beach. Must've been a horrible shipwreck! I don't suppose we'll ever know the truth. Why, you can't even speak, poor dear! Well, never mind – after your scrub in the tub, you're fresh as a daisy in a beautiful new frock!

(PRINCE ERIC enters in dashing threads, with GRIMSBY at his side. Seeing ARIEL stops him in his tracks.)

PRINCE ERIC
Well... now I'm the one who's speechless.

GRIMSBY
It's been a long time since we dined in the company of such loveliness.

PRINCE ERIC
(smiling at ARIEL)
Usually it's just me and Grim. He's gotta look across the table at my ugly mug!

(As GRIMSBY giddily pulls PRINCE ERIC aside downstage for a confidential chat, SEBASTIAN enters opposite, scampers upstage, and hides near ARIEL.)

GRIMSBY
The bath certainly worked its wonders. Your mystery guest is groomed for a groom, you might say!

(CHEF LOUIS enters wielding a serving fork. ARIEL points him in the wrong direction to protect her friend but grabs his fork as he exits. GRIMSBY and PRINCE ERIC do not notice this commotion.)

PRINCE ERIC
(under his breath)
Easy, old boy, easy... She has no voice.

GRIMSBY
Oh, oh dear...

(With great skill, ARIEL starts to comb her hair with the "dinglehopper.")

PRINCE ERIC
(turning to see ARIEL)
My... isn't that unusual?
(ARIEL blushes and hands the fork to PRINCE ERIC.)
Thank you.

(ARIEL then notices the pipe in Grimsby's pocket.)

GRIMSBY
Don't tell me she's fond of pipes!
(hands ARIEL his pipe)
Can't say I blame you. That's an antique from Dusseldorf—

(ARIEL blows into the pipe as though it were a horn – right into GRIMSBY's face. CARLOTTA and PRINCE ERIC laugh.)

PRINCE ERIC
Sorry old friend, but it looks like your pipe smoked you—

GRIMSBY
Very amusing, yes. Well, she certainly knows how to make you smile.

CARLOTTA
Come along, Grimsby. Let's leave the young ones alone for a bit.

(CARLOTTA and GRIMSBY exit.)

PRINCE ERIC
You should see the princesses that Grimsby drags to dinner. So prim, so boring. But you...
(ARIEL grins. PRINCE ERIC stares at her a moment. Then he holds his throat and asks:)
So if you don't mind my asking... what was it? An accident, when you were small?
(ARIEL turns away in shame.)
Oh, I'm sorry, I didn't mean— Who needs words anyway? A smile says just as much sometimes.

(ARIEL smiles again and flexes up and down on her toes.
#30 – ONE STEP CLOSER.*)*

One Step Closer

(PRINCE ERIC): You're nimble on your feet, aren't you? Well, dancing beats small talk any day. It's the way your legs smile... or laugh. It lets you say so many things.

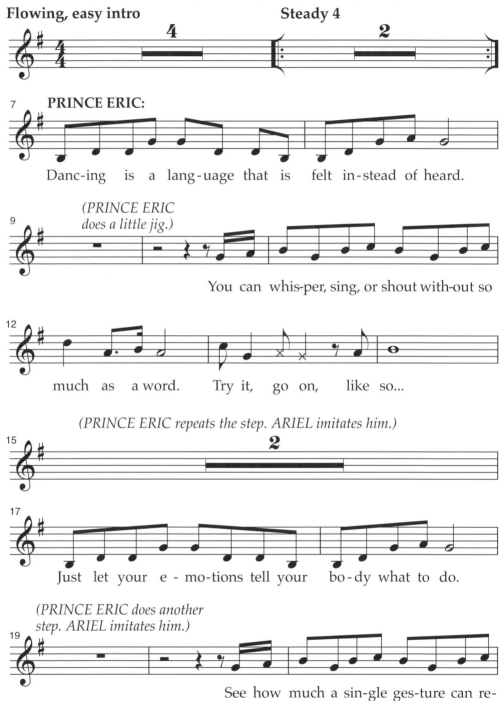

Flowing, easy intro **Steady 4**

PRINCE ERIC:

Danc-ing is a lang-uage that is felt in-stead of heard.

(PRINCE ERIC does a little jig.)

You can whis-per, sing, or shout with-out so

much as a word. Try it, go on, like so...

(PRINCE ERIC repeats the step. ARIEL imitates him.)

Just let your e - mo-tions tell your bo-dy what to do.

(PRINCE ERIC does another step. ARIEL imitates him.)

See how much a sin-gle ges-ture can re-

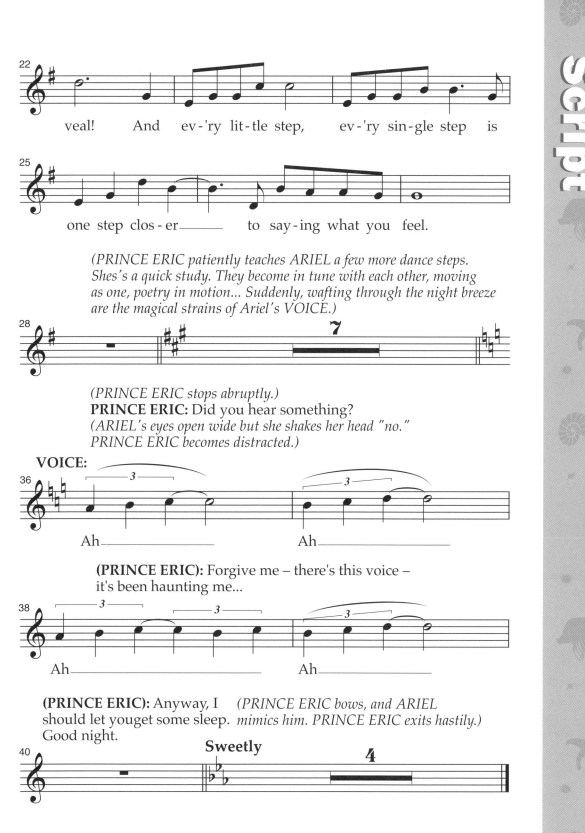

veal! And ev-'ry lit-tle step, ev-'ry sin-gle step is

one step clos-er———— to say-ing what you feel.

(PRINCE ERIC patiently teaches ARIEL a few more dance steps. Shes's a quick study. They become in tune with each other, moving as one, poetry in motion... Suddenly, wafting through the night breeze are the magical strains of Ariel's VOICE.)

(PRINCE ERIC stops abruptly.)
PRINCE ERIC: Did you hear something?
(ARIEL's eyes open wide but she shakes her head "no." PRINCE ERIC becomes distracted.)

VOICE:

Ah———————— Ah————————

(PRINCE ERIC): Forgive me – there's this voice – it's been haunting me...

Ah———————— Ah————————

(PRINCE ERIC): Anyway, I   *(PRINCE ERIC bows, and ARIEL*
should let youget some sleep.   *mimics him. PRINCE ERIC exits hastily.)*
Good night.
Sweetly

(ARIEL, crestfallen, watches him depart. SEBASTIAN emerges from hiding.)

SEBASTIAN

Out of the frying pan, into the fire! The things I do for you, young lady! Now, I should march you right back home to your father—

(ARIEL's eyes grow wide, and she shakes her head "no.")

(SEBASTIAN)

... so you can be miserable the rest of your life...
(sighs heavily, shakes head, gives in)
It's true. I got no backbone... All right, child. I'm in. But we got to get that boy to kiss you before it's too late! Now, a few pointers from a clever crab to a little mermaid. You gotta bat your eyes, like this... Then you gotta pucker your lips, like this...

(SEBASTIAN demonstrates; ARIEL copies.)

(SEBASTIAN)

Oh, that's good!
(exiting with ARIEL)
You put those two things together tomorrow and you got that boy in the palm of your hand...

SCENE FIFTEEN: THE LAGOON

*(#31 – **THE LAGOON**. The SEA CHORUS reconfigures to form a beautiful lagoon, full of enchanting ANIMALS. It is the next evening. PRINCE ERIC and ARIEL enter in a small dinghy, drifting in gentle water. SEBASTIAN and SCUTTLE enter and look on from nearby.)*

PRINCE ERIC

No girl's ever dared to join me out here. Too afraid they'd muddy their shoes. But not you!
(ARIEL beams.)
Peaceful, isn't it? Not another living soul for miles and miles. If only...

(PRINCE ERIC looks away, out into the distance. FLOUNDER emerges.)

FLOUNDER

Hi there! What's happening?

SCUTTLE

Nothing is happening!

SEBASTIAN
(grabs SCUTTLE's beak in his claw)
Shh! They spent all morning on horseback, then an afternoon picnic,
now this... and not so much as a peck on the cheek!

FLOUNDER
Oh no! There's only one day left!

(ARIEL smiles at PRINCE ERIC. He smiles politely back.)

PRINCE ERIC
(awkwardly)
So... how 'bout this weather?

SEBASTIAN
We gotta do something, and quick.

SCUTTLE
But what?

FLOUNDER
This could be our last chance!

SEBASTIAN
We got to create the right kinda mood.

SCUTTLE
You mean like candlelight and champagne?

(FLOTSAM and JETSAM enter to spy on the gathering.)

SEBASTIAN
Nonsense. It don't take all that. Everything we need, we got right here.
(enlisting the ANIMALS as a calypso band)
Percussion...

(#**32 – KISS THE GIRL**.)

Kiss the Girl

(SEBASTIAN): strings... winds... words...

Romantic Calypso

SEBASTIAN:

There you see —her, sit-ting there a-cross the way.

ANIMALS:

mp Sha la la   Sha la la

(SEBASTIAN):

She don't got a lot to say,— but there's some-thing a-bout her.

(SEBASTIAN):

And you don't know why, but you're

ANIMALS:

...a-bout her.

dy-ing to try, you wan-na kiss the girl.—

Kiss the girl.—

Yes, you want her.

Yes, you want her.

Look at her, you know you do.

Look at her, you know you do.

SEBASTIAN:
Pos-si-ble she want you, too. There is one way to

(SEBASTIAN):
ask her. It don't take a word, not a

GROUP 2: **ANIMALS:**
Kiss the girl. Oh, not a

GROUP 1:
Kiss the girl.

(PRINCE ERIC): Maybe I could guess? Alexandra? Annabelle? Beatrice?

hoo   hoo   hoo   hoo   hoo

Kiss her!

PRINCE ERIC: ... Ariel?
(ARIEL shakes her head "yes.")

SEBASTIAN:

A - ri - el.   Her name is   A - ri - el.

(GROUP 1):

hoo⸻   Hoo   hoo

(GROUP 2):

You wan - na   kiss   the girl.

(PRINCE ERIC): <u>Ariel!</u> Hey, that's kinda pretty. Okay – Ariel...
(ARIEL begins to implement Sebastian's puckering advice.)

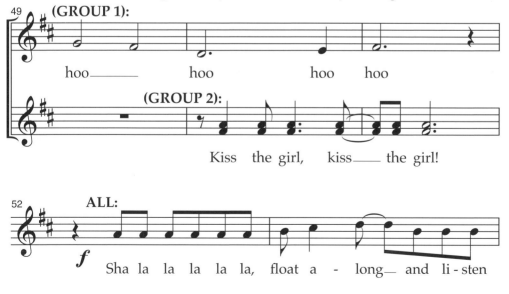

(GROUP 1):

hoo⸻   hoo   hoo   hoo

(GROUP 2):

Kiss   the girl,   kiss⸻ the girl!

ALL:

f   Sha la la la la la, float a - long⸻ and li - sten

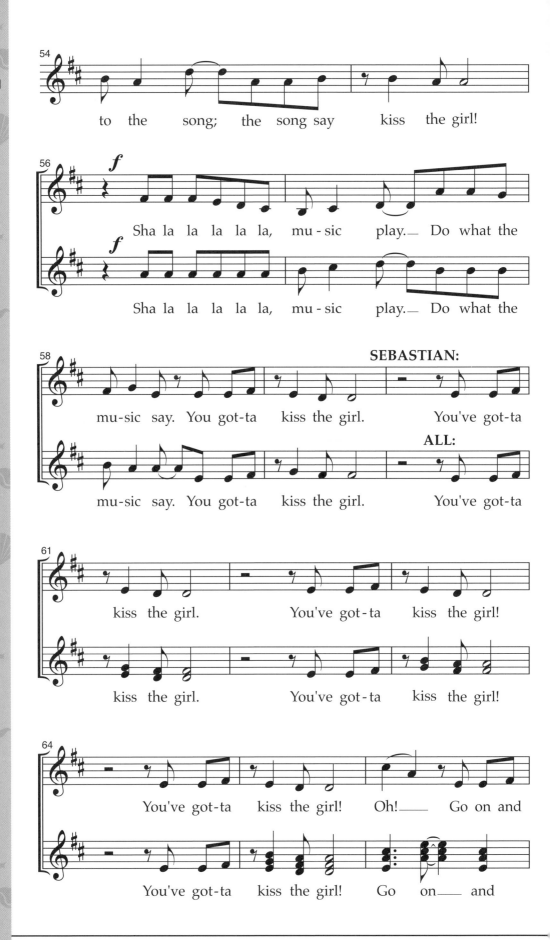

to the song; the song say kiss the girl!

f Sha la la la la la, mu-sic play.— Do what the

f Sha la la la la la, mu-sic play.— Do what the

SEBASTIAN:

mu-sic say. You got-ta kiss the girl. You've got-ta

ALL:

mu-sic say. You got-ta kiss the girl. You've got-ta

kiss the girl. You've got-ta kiss the girl!

kiss the girl. You've got-ta kiss the girl!

You've got-ta kiss the girl! Oh!___ Go on and

You've got-ta kiss the girl! Go on___ and

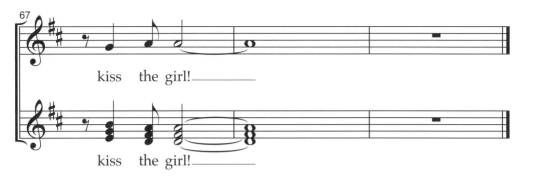

kiss   the girl!⸻

kiss   the girl!⸻

(The song has worked its magic. At long last, PRINCE ERIC leans in to kiss ARIEL.)

JETSAM

Oh, no you don't!

FLOTSAM

Quickly! Block that kiss!

> *(#**33 – ZZZAP!** FLOTSAM and JETSAM knock the boat and shock all the ANIMALS with their electricity. The ANIMALS make a commotion as they scatter and exit.)*

PRINCE ERIC

Whoa! What happened???
> *(steadies the rocking boat with the oars)*

Ariel, are you all right?
> *(ARIEL nods, but inside she is crushed. PRINCE ERIC starts rowing.)*

Well, we ought to get back anyway. Gotta rest up for my birthday tomorrow! Ol' Grimsby's planning a ball to help me find the girl with that voice... He wants me married by sunset, or else!

> *(#**34 – KISS THE GIRL – PLAYOFF**. ARIEL allows a tear to escape, but she smiles for PRINCE ERIC's sake as they exit.)*

SCENE SIXTEEN: THE PALACE HALL

(The SEA CHORUS dissolves the lagoon and reconfigures to form the palace hall. ARIEL enters with CARLOTTA.)

CARLOTTA
Oh, Ariel dearest, I can't believe you've been with us three whole days already! It's been such a treat!
(ARIEL smiles gratefully at CARLOTTA.)
Now, the princesses are arriving to sing for Prince Eric so he can finally choose his bride! You just stand back here with Carlotta while the royalty mingles. It's sure to be quite a show!

(GRIMSBY enters, followed by PRINCE ERIC. #35 – THE CONTEST.)

The Contest

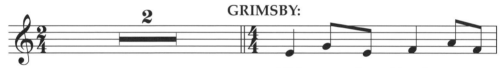

(As GRIMSBY calls the gathering to order, opportunistic PRINCESSES parade in, escorted by groomed SAILORS. ARIEL is crushed.)

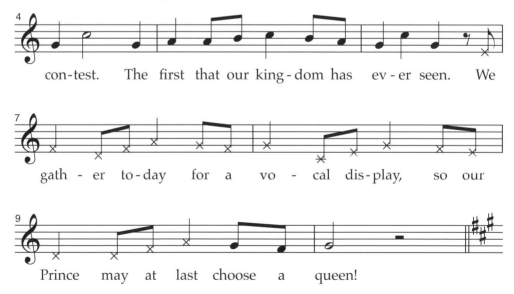

GRIMSBY: Wel-come, dear friends, to our con-test. The first that our king-dom has ev-er seen. We gath-er to-day for a vo-cal dis-play, so our Prince may at last choose a queen!

GRIMSBY: These six Princesses possess the most accomplished voices in the land! *(to the PRINCESSES)* Tonight, one of you will join Prince Eric on the throne. May the best woman win! *(One by one, the PRINCESSES step forward to sing.)*

GRIMSBY: Surely one of these lovely voices matches the music in your heart—
PRINCE ERIC: *(unconvinced and disheartened)* I wish I could say "yes"! But she's not here.

GRIMSBY: The sun has nearly set, and your birthday will soon be over. You must choose a mate!

(Aware that this is her last chance, ARIEL forces her way into the center of the hall.)

PRINCE ERIC

Ariel?

CARLOTTA

(hopeful, to ARIEL)
Oh, dear one.

GRIMSBY

For heaven's sake, child—

PRINCE ERIC

Quiet, Grimsby. Go ahead, Ariel.

(ARIEL takes a deep breath. #36 – ONE STEP CLOSER – REPRISE. It looks as if she's about to attempt a note. But instead, ARIEL executes a few of the dance steps PRINCE ERIC taught her two nights earlier. The PRINCESSES laugh. ARIEL looks to PRINCE ERIC, helpless, then runs into CARLOTTA's arms.)

CARLOTTA

Oh, child! Poor, lost child.

GRIMSBY

I had so hoped, dear Eric, that you might find love somewhere in this room.

PRINCE ERIC

(smiling)
I have, Grimsby. I've just been too blind to see it... until now. Come here, Ariel.

(# 37 – TIME'S UP. PRINCE ERIC takes a knee. Suddenly, wafting on the breeze: URSULA has unleashed ARIEL's true VOICE yet again.)

Time's Up

GRIMSBY: Can it be? Another contestant?

PRINCE ERIC: *(jumping up)* That's the voice! *(ARIEL looks at him, panicked.)* But— but tell her the competition is over. I've already made my choice. *(ARIEL beams. PRINCE ERIC takes her hand.)*

(Just then the sun sets. The lyrical VOICE morphs into a sinister rattle:)

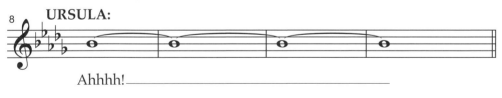

URSULA: Why look! Such a gorgeous sunset! And on the third day, too! Time's up. You lose!

(Now turning back into a mermaid, ARIEL begins to stumble and gasp for air.)
PRINCE ERIC: Ariel, what's wrong?
(A magic force pulls ARIEL offstage. SEBASTIAN follows her.)
SEBASTIAN: Oh no. The worst is happening. I've got to get help!
(SEBASTIAN exits.)

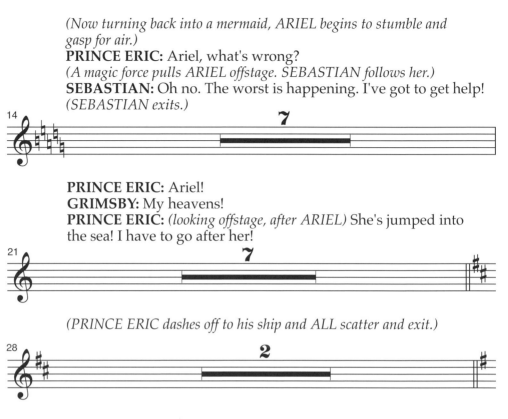

PRINCE ERIC: Ariel!
GRIMSBY: My heavens!
PRINCE ERIC: *(looking offstage, after ARIEL)* She's jumped into the sea! I have to go after her!

(PRINCE ERIC dashes off to his ship and ALL scatter and exit.)

SCENE SEVENTEEN: ARIEL'S GROTTO

(The SEA CHORUS dissolves the palace, "descends" into the ocean, and forms the ruins of Ariel's grotto.)

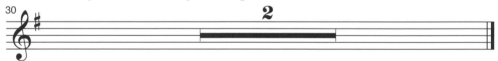

KING TRITON

Ariel?!? I haven't seen you for three days and I'm... worried. I thought you might be here... Ariel? I've – I've come to apologize...

(SEBASTIAN and FLOUNDER enter.)

SEBASTIAN

Most merciful Triton—

KING TRITON

Where have you been, Sebastian? <u>And where is Ariel?</u>

SEBASTIAN

Oh, she'd be so angry if she knew I was here—

KING TRITON

I entrust my youngest daughter to you, and what happens? <u>She disappears</u>! I ought to have you cracked and shelled!

FLOUNDER

He almost was, Your Greatness.

KING TRITON

What kind of tragedy will it take—

SEBASTIAN

(cowering, can barely squeak it out)
A tragedy involving the Sea Witch...

KING TRITON

What?!?

FLOUNDER

(to himself)
Don't be a guppy. Don't be a guppy.
(to KING TRITON)
You see, Your Majesty, these two slippery eels came and took Ariel to Ursula, and she traded her voice for a pair of legs—

KING TRITON

She bartered away <u>her voice</u> to become <u>human</u>?!?

SEBASTIAN

Yes. And now that child has given up her very soul—

KING TRITON

(looking up, hopelessly)
Oh, Ariel! What have you done??
(to SEBASTIAN and FLOUNDER, with resolve)
Come, we must save my daughter!

(KING TRITON, SEBASTIAN, and FLOUNDER dash off to
#38 – URSULA'S LAIR.*)*

SCENE EIGHTEEN: URSULA'S LAIR

(The SEA CHORUS forms Ursula's lair. URSULA enters, her TENTACLES in a tizzy. FLOTSAM and JETSAM enter with ARIEL, who has regained her tail. She struggles in the EELS' electric grip.)

URSULA

Say goodbye to your prince! You're mine now, <u>mermaid</u>! Get ready to spend the rest of your days as my slave!

(Ursula's TENTACLES begin to wrap around ARIEL. KING TRITON enters, followed by SEBASTIAN and FLOUNDER.)

KING TRITON

Ursula!

URSULA

King Triton! You're right on cue!

KING TRITON

What have you done to my daughter?

URSULA

Nothing! She's done it all to herself, trading her voice away. And for what? Human heartbreak!

KING TRITON

Give her back to me.

URSULA

Not on your life!

(#39 – <u>POOR UNFORTUNATE SOULS – REPRISE</u>.)

Poor Unfortunate Souls (Reprise)

URSULA:
It so hap-pens that your daugh-ter made a

KING TRITON:
No!
bar-gain. Swapped her voice to land a man up where it's

dry.   Is it bind-ing? Good-ness, yes!   Un -

KING TRITON:
Unless?

break-a-ble, un-less... There   is a lit-tle some-thin' we could

KING TRITON:
Go on.

try.   Yes... per-haps we could ar-range a   sort of

trade-off.   May-be swap your daugh-ter's soul for, say, your

KING TRITON:
What?

own.   Make this   deal and set her   free,   or

else she comes with me,   to   suf-fer through e-ter-ni-ty a-

KING TRITON: It's not my soul you're after –
(holds up his trident) – it's my power.

lone...

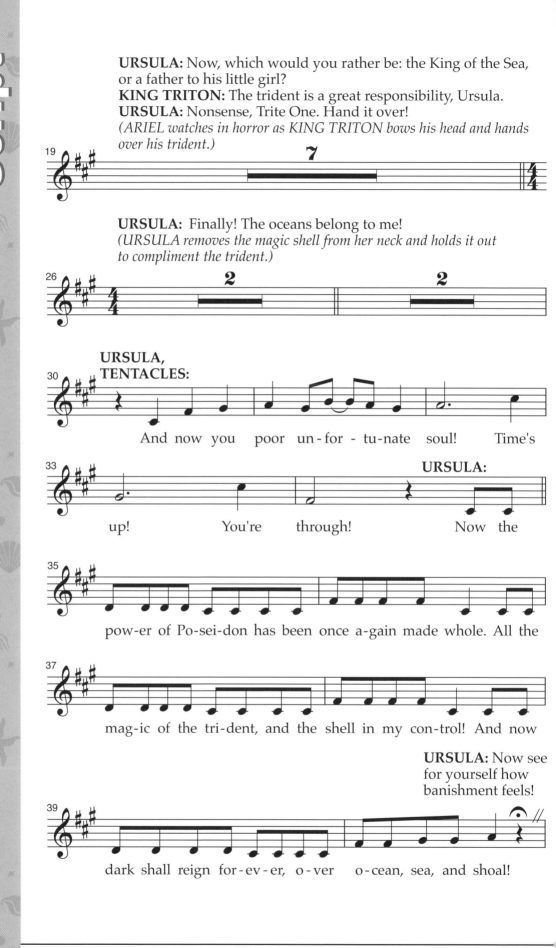

URSULA: Now, which would you rather be: the King of the Sea, or a father to his little girl?

KING TRITON: The trident is a great responsibility, Ursula.

URSULA: Nonsense, Trite One. Hand it over!

(ARIEL watches in horror as KING TRITON bows his head and hands over his trident.)

URSULA: Finally! The oceans belong to me!

(URSULA removes the magic shell from her neck and holds it out to compliment the trident.)

URSULA, TENTACLES:
And now you poor un-for-tu-nate soul! Time's up! You're through!

URSULA:
Now the pow-er of Po-sei-don has been once a-gain made whole. All the mag-ic of the tri-dent, and the shell in my con-trol! And now

URSULA: Now see for yourself how banishment feels!

dark shall reign for-ev-er, o-ver o-cean, sea, and shoal!

(URSULA aims the trident and blasts KING TRITON offstage. The TENTACLES begin to stretch out, making URSULA grow larger.)

URSULA, FLOTSAM, JETSAM, TENTACLES:

You poor un - for-tu-nate soul!

SCENE NINETEEN: THE OCEAN SURFACE

(As URSULA cackles and points the trident skyward, she grows enormous with power, her TENTACLES "grabbing" FLOUNDER, SEBASTIAN, ARIEL, FLOTSAM, and JETSAM. The SEA CHORUS "ascends" with them and forms the surface of the ocean. Prince Eric's ship approaches with PRINCE ERIC and the PILOT.)
PRINCE ERIC: You there!

(#40 – CONFRONTATION.)

Confrontation

URSULA, TENTACLES:
What's this? A human ship?
TENTACLES: Ha!

PRINCE ERIC: Who are you?
And what have you done with Ariel?
URSULA: Careful, princey-poo!
The water's looking awfully choppy!

(URSULA points the trident to rile the seas. Her TENTACLES menacingly poke out of the surface.)
PILOT: Beware, monster! King Triton rules over these seas!
URSULA: Not anymore!

PRINCE ERIC: I won't let you harm her!
URSULA: Ha!
(URSULA and the TENTACLES cackle and reach toward the ship.)
PILOT: Captain, we've got to turn back, or she'll pull us under!

(With URSULA distracted by PRINCE ERIC, ARIEL snatches the magic shell from URSULA's grasp and holds it high above her head.)
FLOTSAM: Look out!
JETSAM: The shell!
URSULA, TENTACLES: *(to ARIEL)* You fool!

(Shocked by this turn of events, the TENTACLES release their grasp on FLOUNDER, SEBASTIAN, ARIEL, FLOTSAM, and JETSAM.)
FLOUNDER: *(a guppy no more, charges URSULA)* You witch!
FLOTSAM: *(apprehending FLOUNDER)* Not so fast, guppy!

JETSAM: *(charging ARIEL)* Get the shell!
SEBASTIAN: *(apprehending JETSAM)* Stop there, sea-snake!
(FLOTSAM restrains FLOUNDER as SEBASTIAN clamps JETSAM – a sidekick stalemate. The action freezes as URSULA witnesses her most prized possession, the magic shell, glow in ARIEL's hands and release the voice back into her larynx:)

ARIEL:

Ah

ARIEL: *(touching her throat)* My voice...
URSULA: Well... look who's talking! No matter. *(shakes the trident)* I have what I want now. And you don't!

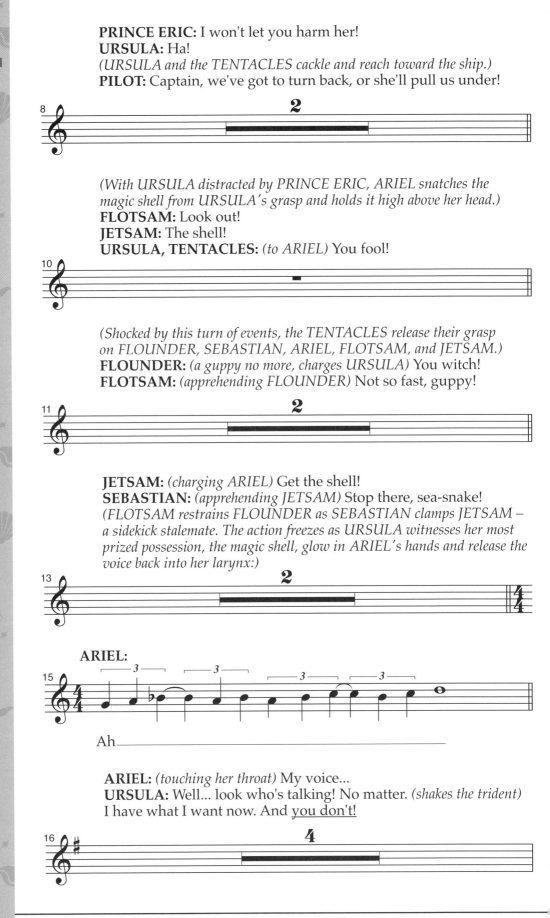

(The TENTACLES pull ARIEL face-to-face with URSULA. URSULA aims the trident at ARIEL, but ARIEL doesn't flinch.)
ARIEL: You may have my father's trident, but you'll never have his power.

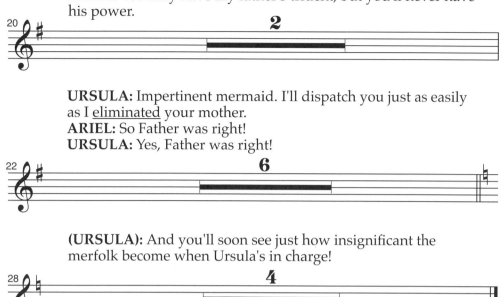

URSULA: Impertinent mermaid. I'll dispatch you just as easily as I <u>eliminated</u> your mother.
ARIEL: So Father was right!
URSULA: Yes, Father was right!

(URSULA): And you'll soon see just how insignificant the merfolk become when Ursula's in charge!

(URSULA)

With trident in hand, I shall unleash the power of Poseidon to <u>destroy you all</u>!

*(**#41 – WHIRLPOOL**. As URSULA points the trident at the waters and makes circling motions, the SEA CHORUS forms a whirlpool around her, but it soon gets out of control. URSULA and the TENTACLES begin spinning as well.)*

(URSULA)

Wait. Oh, no. Stop. I – I can't control it!

SEBASTIAN

Ariel, the trident!

(ARIEL breaks free of the TENTACLES' grasp and bravely reaches out to grab the trident. ARIEL extends the trident to SEBASTIAN and FLOUNDER, who grab hold and stay afloat while the sea swallows URSULA, the TENTACLES, and FLOTSAM and JETSAM.)

URSULA, TENTACLES, FLOTSAM, JETSAM

Noooooo!

(With URSULA's reign of terror now over, the SEA CHORUS becomes calm around ARIEL, SEBASTIAN, and FLOUNDER.)

SEBASTIAN

Ariel! Are you all right, child?

ARIEL

Yes. Thank you for your help.

FLOUNDER

Not such a guppy any more, am I?

ARIEL

Nope. You're the best friends a girl could wish for.

> *(SEBASTIAN and FLOUNDER embrace ARIEL. KING TRITON breaks through the surface, now free from his imprisonment.)*

KING TRITON

Ariel!

ARIEL

Daddy!
> *(hands KING TRITON the trident and bows her head)*
I've caused so much trouble. Can you ever forgive me?

KING TRITON

Why, I've never been prouder. Somehow, in the blink of an eye, when my back was turned, you grew up.
> *(hugs ARIEL, who looks out toward the land)*
You love him very much, don't you?

> *(ARIEL nods. **#42 – HUMAN AGAIN**. As KING TRITON waves his trident – with much more control and grace than Ursula demonstrated – the SEA CHORUS peacefully encircles ARIEL. KING TRITON moves the seas toward the land.)*

Human Again

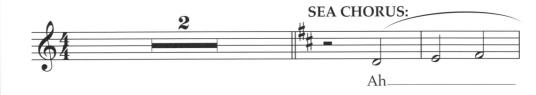

SCENE TWENTY: THE BEACH

*(The SEA CHORUS forms the beach and parts the waters.
KING TRITON places the newly human ARIEL on the sand.)*

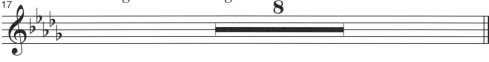

KING TRITON: You belong to his world now.
ARIEL: Thank you, Daddy. Thank you so much.
KING TRITON: Just remember... when you hear the surf roar
at night and feel the tingle of salt in the air... it's only your father,
checking in on his little girl.

(PRINCE ERIC bounds in, followed by GRIMSBY.)

PRINCE ERIC

Ariel!
    (stops short, seeing KING TRITON)
Who are you?

KING TRITON

I'm her father, King Triton. And you're the human who came to her
rescue.

PRINCE ERIC

    (in awe)
With all due respect, sir, Ariel is the one who has done the rescuing.

GRIMSBY
(can't believe his eyes)
The King of the Sea? And she's his <u>daughter</u>?

PRINCE ERIC
Does that upset you?

GRIMSBY
Heavens, no! I'm just relieved she's royalty!

PRINCE ERIC
(to KING TRITON)
Your Majesty? At last, I've found someone who makes me eager to seize the future and claim my birthright as king.
(looks at ARIEL)
But if I slip out to sea sometimes, I hope she'll be right there beside me.
(to KING TRITON)
May I have her hand?

KING TRITON
Ariel can speak for herself.

PRINCE ERIC
She can?

(#43 – <u>PART OF YOUR WORLD – FINALE</u>.)

Part of Your World (Finale)

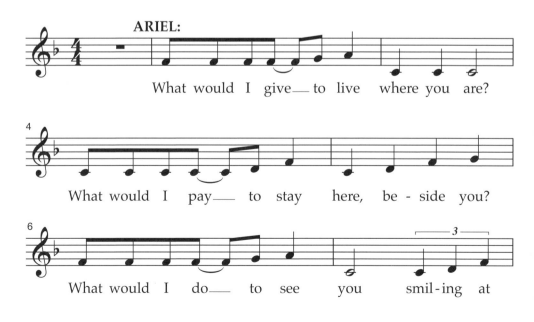

ARIEL:
What would I give— to live where you are?

What would I pay— to stay here, be - side you?

What would I do— to see you smil - ing at

PRINCE ERIC: *(smiling wide)* Oh, Ariel!
It's been <u>your voice</u> all along!
(PRINCE ERIC and ARIEL embrace at last.)

(#44 – UNDER THE SEA – BOWS.)

Under the Sea (Bows)

Buoyant Calypso beat

Un-der the sea, un - der the sea. No - bod-y beat us, fry— us, and eat us in— fric-a - see. We— what the land folks love— to cook. Un - der the sea we off— the hook. Each lit-tle snail here know— how to wail here. That's why it's hot-ter un - der the wa-ter. Ya, we in

luck here   down   in   the   muck here,   un - der   the

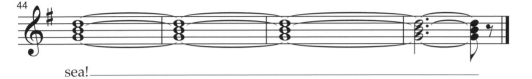

sea!

(#45 – EXIT MUSIC.)

Actor's Glossary

actor: A person who performs as a character in a play or musical.

antagonist: A person who actively opposes the protagonist.

author: A writer of a play; also known as a playwright. A musical's authors include a book writer, a composer, and a lyricist.

blocking: The actors' movements around the stage in a play or musical, not including the choreography. The director usually "blocks" the show (or assigns blocking) during rehearsals.

book writer: One of the authors of a musical. The book writer writes the lines of dialogue and the stage directions. A book writer can be called a librettist if she writes the lyrics as well.

cast: The performers in a show.

cheating out: Turning slightly toward the house when performing so the audience can better see one's face and hear one's lines.

choreographer: A person who creates and teaches the dance numbers in a musical.

choreography: The dances in a musical that are often used to help tell the story.

composer: A person who writes music for a musical.

creative team: The director, choreographer, music director, and designers working on a production. The original creative team for a musical also includes the author(s) and orchestrator.

cross: An actor's movement to a new position onstage.

dialogue: A conversation between two or more characters.

director: A person who provides the artistic vision, coordinates the creative elements, and stages the play.

downstage: The portion of the stage closest to the audience; the opposite of upstage.

house: The area of the theater where the audience sits to watch the show.

house left: The left side of the theater from the audience's perspective.

house right: The right side of the theater from the audience's perspective.

librettist: The person who writes both dialogue and lyrics for a musical. Can also be referred to separately as the book writer and lyricist.

libretto: A term referring to the script (dialogue and stage directions) and lyrics together.

lines: The dialogue spoken by the actors.

lyricist: A person who writes the lyrics, or sung words, of a musical. The lyricist works with a composer to create songs.

lyrics: The words of a song.

monologue: A large block of lines spoken by a single character.

music director: A person in charge of teaching the songs to the cast and orchestra and maintaining the quality of the performed score. The music director may also conduct a live orchestra during performances.

musical: A play that incorporates music and choreography to tell a story.

objective: What a character wants to do or achieve.

off-book: An actor's ability to perform memorized lines without holding the script.

offstage: Any area out of view of the audience; also called backstage.

onstage: Anything on the stage within view of the audience.

opening night: The first official performance of a production, after which the show is frozen, meaning no further changes are made.

play: A type of dramatic writing meant to be performed live on a stage. A musical is one kind of play.

protagonist: The main character of a story on which the action is centered.

raked stage: A stage that is raised slightly upstage so that it slants toward the audience.

read-through: An early rehearsal of a play at which actors read their dialogue from scripts without blocking or memorized lines.

rehearsal: A meeting during which the cast learns and practices the show.

score: All musical elements of a show, including songs and underscoring.

script: 1) The written words that make up a show, including dialogue, stage directions, and lyrics. 2) The book that contains those words.

speed-through: To perform the dialogue of a scene as quickly as possible. A speed-through rehearsal helps actors memorize their lines and infuses energy into the pacing of a scene.

stage directions: Words in the script that describe character actions that are not part of the dialogue.

stage left: The left side of the stage, from the actor's perspective.

stage manager: A person responsible for keeping all rehearsals and performances organized and on schedule.

stage right: The right side of the stage, from the actor's perspective.

upstage: The part of the stage farthest from the audience; the opposite of downstage.

warm-ups: Exercises at the beginning of a rehearsal or before a performance that prepare actors' voices and bodies.

Show Glossary

ah mais oui: (ah may wee) French phrase meaning "oh, but yes."

attention: (ah-TEN-see-yon) French word meaning "attention."

bartered: Traded good or services for other goods or services without using money.

bonjour: (bon-JOOR) French word meaning "hello" or "good day."

ça c'est toujours: (sa say too-JOOR) French phrase meaning "it is always."

curried: Prepared or flavored with a sauce of curry or other hot spices.

dinghy: Small, open boat with a mast and sails.

droll: Curious or unusual in mildly amusing manner.

escargot: (es-kar-GOH) A French delicacy made up of cooked land snails.

fathom: A unit of measurement used specifically to measure depth of water; one fathom is the same distance as two yards or six feet.

fish fillet: (fil-LAY) A thinly cut slice of boneless fish.

fish *flambé*: (flahm-BAY) A French dish prepared by spreading brandy over the meal and igniting it to create a dramatic presentation.

fish *pâté*: (pah-TAY) A fancy dish of ground fish made into a spread and served with bread.

fricasee: A popular Cajun stewed dish made with seafood, gravy, and vegetables.

kippered: A preparation of fish by salting and drying it in open air.

lobster bisque: (beesk) A creamy soup made with lobster and vegetables.

le menu: (luh Meh-NIEW) French phrase meaning "the menu."

maintenant: (meh-tuh-NAH) French word meaning "now."

les poissons: (lay Pwa-SOHN) French phrase meaning "the fish."

pour çe soir: (poor seh swar) French phrase meaning "for this evening."

roustabout: An unskilled or casual worker.

sashimi: A Japanese dish with very fresh fish, sliced into thin pieces and served with rice.

tuna tartare: (tar-TAR) A dish made from finely chopped fish that is seasoned and served on toast.

vendetta: A bitter, prolonged quarrel with someone or a group of people.

zut alors: (zoot a-LOHR) A French expression meaning "Oh my goodness!"

Credits & Copyrights

1. Orchestra Tune-Up
2. Fathoms Below* – music by Alan Menken, lyrics by Glenn Slater
3. Triton's Court* – music by Alan Menken
4. Sebastian's Fanfare* – music by Alan Menken
5. Daughters of Triton° – music by Alan Menken, lyrics by Howard Ashman
6. Where's Ariel?° – music by Alan Menken, lyrics by Howard Ashman
7. The Beach† – music by Alan Menken
8. Finding Scuttle• – music by Alan Menken
9. Human Stuff˘ – music by Alan Menken, lyrics by Glenn Slater
10. Human Stuff (Playoff) / Into Ursula's Lair• – music by Alan Menken
11. Into King Triton's Court• – music by Alan Menken
12. Part of Your World° – music by Alan Menken, lyrics by Howard Ashman
13. Under the Sea° – music by Alan Menken, lyrics by Howard Ashman
14. Under the Sea (Playoff)° – music by Alan Menken
15. Prince Eric's Ship‡ – music by Alan Menken
16. The Storm‡ – music by Alan Menken
17. Part of Your World (Reprise 1)° – music by Alan Menken, lyrics by Howard Ashman
18. Part of Your World (Reprise 2)° – music by Alan Menken, lyrics by Howard Ashman
19. She's in Love˘ – music by Alan Menken, lyrics by Glenn Slater
20. Flounder Flounders˘ – music by Alan Menken
21. Ariel's Grotto† – music Alan Menken
22. Grotto Destruction
23. Murky Waters* – music by Alan Menken
24. Poor Unfortunate Souls° – music by Alan Menken, lyrics by Howard Ashman
25. Beluga Sevruga° – music by Alan Menken, lyrics by Howard Ashman
26. Eric Enters† – music Alan Menken
27. The Palace Kitchen* – music by Alan Menken
28. Les Poissons* – music by Alan Menken, lyrics by Howard Ashman & Glenn Slater
29. The Palace Hall˘ – music by Alan Menken
30. One Step Closer˘ – music by Alan Menken, lyrics by Glenn Slater
31. The Lagoon˘ – music by Alan Menken
32. Kiss the Girl° – music by Alan Menken, lyrics by Howard Ashman
33. Zzzap!
34. Kiss the Girl (Playoff)° – music by Alan Menken
35. The Contest* – music by Alan Menken, lyrics by Glenn Slater
36. One Step Closer (Reprise)˘ – music by Alan Menken
37. Time's Up† – music Alan Menken
38. Ursula's Lair† – music Alan Menken
39. Poor Unfortunate Souls (Reprise)˘ – music by Alan Menken, lyrics by Glenn Slater
40. Confrontation˘ – music by Alan Menken
41. Whirlpool˘ – music by Alan Menken
42. Human Again˘ – music by Alan Menken
43. Part of Your World (Finale)° – music by Alan Menken, lyrics by Howard Ashman
44. Under the Sea (Bows)° – music by Alan Menken, lyrics by Howard Ashman
45. Exit Music˘ – music by Alan Menken

The Little Mermaid JR. is based on the 2008 Broadway production of
The Little Mermaid, produced by Disney Theatrical Productions.

Original Broadway Orchestrations by
Danny Troob

Original Broadway Incidental Music and Vocal Arrangements by
Michael Kosarin

Original Broadway Dance Arrangements by
David Chase

***The Little Mermaid JR.* Music Adapted and Arranged by**
David Weinstein

***The Little Mermaid JR.* Script Adapted by**
Ken Cerniglia

ShowKit® Content
Disney Theatrical Group: Ken Cerniglia, Lauren Chapman, Matt Hagmeier Curtis,
Julie Haverkate, Rachel Lee, Lisa Mitchell, Colleen McCormack, David Redman Scott
Disney Teaching Artists: Dierdre Friel, Jodi Gelbman,
Angela Jamieson, Jamie Kalama Wood, James Miles, Annie Montgomery, LeeAnet
Noble, Christopher Peterson, Erin Ronder, Heidi Stallings
iTheatrics: Diane Clune, Susan Fuller, Timothy Allen McDonald, Marty Johnson,
Cynthia A. Ripley, Rob Rokicki, Lindsay Lupi

Designers
Steven G. Kennedy, Kevin Johnson, Kevin Yates

**The Broadway Junior® Concept and Format
created by Music Theatre International (MTI)**

Adaptation and support materials developed for MTI by iTheatrics
under the supervision of Timothy Allen McDonald.

Find a complete list of Broadway Junior® musicals at **broadwayjr.com**.
School Edition and full-length musicals may be found at **MTIShows.com**.
Disney stage titles may be found at **DisneyTheatricalLicensing.com**.

@DisneyMusicals   @DisneyOnYourStage